# PRAISE FOR THE BOOKS OF
#### #1 INTERNATIONAL BESTSELLING AUTHOR
# KERK MURRAY

### *Little Black Dog*

"Okay so I literally never leave reviews but I HAVE to for this one. This is THE best dog book. Max reminds me so much of my Winston."

— Reader Review

"As someone who lost my beagle last spring, I approached this book with caution. I'm glad I read it. It was more than what I expected."

— Reader Review

"I was lucky enough to get an early copy and I've already read it twice."

— Reader Review

### *Since the Day We Promised*

"Books don't often make me sob, but this one did. There was an innocence and nostalgia about the story that gave me all the feels."
— Reader Review

"I have only two words for this series and this book in particular. Absolutely amazing!"
— Reader Review

"What a finale. I am glad to have read and enjoyed all six books."
— Reader Review

### *Since the Day We Left*

"Haven't cried that hard over a book in a long time."
— Reader Review

## *Since the Day We Wished*

"I hope this gets made into a movie. So good!"

— Reader Review

## *Since the Day We Kissed*

"This is the first romance I've read written by a male and won't be my last by this author. His take on romance was surprisingly insightful—you can't help but cheer for Kara and Ethan."

— Reader Review

"The best story in the series by far!"

— Reader Review

"I can't wait to read more Kerk Murray books! He's my favorite new-to-me author."

— Reader Review

## *Since the Day We Fell*

"Hadley Cove feels like a character in itself. It's a place that feels both real and magical and one that I never want to leave."
— Reader Review


"Kerk has a gift for capturing the nuances of human emotion. I found myself stopping to highlight several passages."
— Reader Review


"I've been a fan of Kerk's work since *Pawprints On Our Hearts*, and *Since the Day We Fell* did not disappoint."
— Reader Review


### *Since the Day We Danced*


"Murray's writing is simply gorgeous."
— The Book Commentary


"An emotional rollercoaster that will make you fall in love with love all over again."
— Reader Review

"A beautiful escapist Nicholas Sparks type romance."

— Reader Review

### *Pawprints On Our Hearts*

"Animal lovers will feel connected to Murray's almost spiritual awakening and admire his devotion to following his heart, even in the face of tremendous sacrifice. This touching memoir overflows with intense emotion."

— Booklife by Publishers Weekly

"A deeply moving memoir... one of the best books that capture the connection between human beings and dogs... *Pawprints on Our Hearts* inspires a love for animals while exploring the painful edges of the human heart in need of love and healing."

— The Book Commentary

"A powerful and emotional story."

— Alyson Sheldrake, Bestselling author of
"Kat the Dog"

# BY KERK MURRAY

## Dog Lovers Series

*Pawprints On Our Hearts*
*Little Black Dog*

## Hadley Cove Sweet Romance Series

*Since the Day We Danced*
*Since the Day We Fell*
*Since the Day We Kissed*
*Since the Day We Wished*
*Since the Day We Left*
*Since the Day We Promised*

## Sugarberry Ridge Holiday Romance Series

*The Christmas Angel*
*The Christmas Star*
*The Christmas Wish*
*The Christmas Miracle*
*The Christmas Train*
*The Christmas Cottage*

# Little
# Black Dog

# Little
# Black Dog

A Story of Love, Laughter,
and Stolen Sandwiches

Dog Lovers: Book 2

# KERK MURRAY

Magnolia Press
Birmingham

Magnolia Press
105 Vulcan Rd
Ste 221
Birmingham, AL 35209

Library of Congress Cataloging-in-Publication Data

Names: Murray, Kerk, author.
Title: Little Black Dog/ Kerk Murray.
Description: First edition. | Birmingham: Magnolia Press, 2025.
Identifiers: LCCN 2025927798 | ISBN 9798992553864 (paperback) | ISBN 9798992553871 (hardcover)

Printed in the United States of America

# Before You Begin...

You're invited to join my private Facebook Reader Group, where you'll make new book friends, meet other animal lovers, and be the first to know about new releases, book clubs, and special deals.

**Join today:**
**Kerk Murray's private Facebook Reader Group**

facebook.com/groups/779562103953550

# Maximus

## Spartacus

To Crystal, Maximus,
and Spartacus—my loves.

# Dear Reader,

If you're holding this book, there's a good chance you've loved an animal in a way that's hard to explain to people who haven't.

I wrote this book because Max asked me to, and also because I didn't want to wait until he was gone to give him his flowers.

Still, all of this wouldn't be possible without you.

Thank you for being here. Thank you for supporting *Pawprints on Our Hearts* and for giving this story a chance too. Your kindness has allowed me to keep writing and to keep giving back to the animals through *The Lexi's Legacy Foundation*. That means more than I can say.

Before I go, Max would like to add something: "If there's any sandwiches near you, they belong to me."

♡ Kerk & Max

"What we have once enjoyed we can never lose. All that we love deeply becomes a part of us."

—Helen Keller, *We Bereaved*

# 1

# Banana Muffins

## August 2025

I'VE SEEN HORROR MOVIES that start in places like this.

I cut the engine and take in the view through the windshield. A black-sided A-frame sits on a deck overlooking Weiss Lake. "We're here."

The words sound more hopeful than I feel. I take a breath and remind myself this is supposed to be relaxing.

There are three non-negotiables when anyone invites me somewhere outdoors: air conditioning, internet access, and a toilet. Miss even one, and it's an automatic no—unless there's a pool. That's the only exception.

Perhaps my disdain for the outdoors originates from growing up in the Georgia heat, spending summers working outside, or those full-gear two-a-day football camps where the humidity made every breath feel like I was gasping through a wet towel. Somewhere along the way, I decided that the "great" outdoors was a lot greater when you were admiring it from behind the window of an air-conditioned room.

I hadn't even heard of "glamping" until a few months ago. When I discovered you could "experience nature" without actually roughing it, I was mostly sold. Through the online booking, this cabin checked all three of my boxes and looked perfect for a joint birthday getaway. But pictures can lie.

*Guess we'll see.*

Beside me, my wife Crystal unbuckles her seat belt. "Think they know?"

I grin. "They know something's up."

In the back seat, two pairs of eyes track our every move. Maximus, our black Yorkipoo, strains against his harness. Spartacus, our white and copper Morkie, sits calm and collected.

Both are buckled in thanks to a Facebook ad featuring a stuffed-animal dog flying through a windshield in slow motion. I'd ordered the harnesses before the video even ended.

Grabbing the keys, I step out of the car and inhale the afternoon air. Well, late afternoon, but surprisingly mild for an Alabama August.

*Small wins.*

We're a month overdue for this party. Both our boys have July birthdays—Spartacus on the ninth, and Maximus on the seventeenth. We call them brothers, though they're not related by blood. But they're brothers in every way that matters. The cabin wasn't available in July, and we'd learned that they don't care about which day their birthdays are celebrated. They care about food and whether or not we're sharing ours with them.

When Crystal opens the passenger rear door, we unclip the dogs' seat tethers, then attach their leashes to their harnesses. It's a necessary step we never skip in open areas like this. Maximus would dart away the second he got the chance. Trust me, we've tested it. Twice. Spartacus would probably wait for permission first. Even so, we don't risk it. "Boys, let's—"

Before she can finish, Max explodes from the backseat. He hits the gravel and immediately yanks me forward, his red leash going taut in my hand. He lunges left, then right, straining toward the cabin, and pulling with everything his sixteen-pound body can muster.

"Maximus Murray." I use his full government name and dig in my heels, reeling him back just enough to keep him still.

I turn and see Crystal carefully lifting Spartacus out of the seat and setting him gently on the ground. Ever since his leg surgery—a torn ligament the vet compared to a human ACL—he's been our fragile one. It happened in our backyard one evening, and when he'd hobbled in on three legs, our hearts had broken. We took him to the vet and tried other alternatives, but nothing seemed to help him until the surgery.

These days, we do our best to prevent him from running too fast or jumping off anything too high. At home, we've strategically placed dog stairs leading up to the couch and even positioned the dog beds nearby to provide extra cushioning in the event of an unsanctioned leap. There have been some scares when he tries to copy his more athletic brother, who I'm convinced has set some kind of small dog world record for highest and longest jump.

Spartacus steps out on his blue leash and stretches his front legs, then back. He sniffs the air, then looks up at Crystal like he's waiting for her approval to move. He's always been a momma's boy, and Max has always been a daddy's boy.

How it ended up this way, we'll never know. Of course we both love each of them and they love us, but there's just something about the way Spartacus gravitates toward Crystal and how Max shadows me. We've never had an official conversation about it, but whenever we're out and about, Crystal is Spartacus's assigned guardian and I'm Max's.

We head toward the deck, and Max pulls me up the wooden stairs as Spartacus walks calmly beside Crystal, pausing once to look out at the lake before continuing.

When we reach the front door, I unlock it and push it open. Cool air brushes my face, carrying a hint of cedar and something floral. We step inside, and it looks just like the photos. Maybe even better.

This place is stocked: a basket of snacks on the counter, an espresso machine beside a rack of coffee pods, and a mini-fridge. There's a microwave, and next to it, a small wooden sign with *Wi-Fi* and *Password* written in neat cursive.

*Promising.*

I squat to remove Max's harness while Crystal does the same for Spartacus. "All right. You're free."

Max charges ahead and vaults from floor to couch to bed in one glorious burst of chaos. The bed bounces, and he uses the momentum to launch himself toward the kitchenette, sliding across the floor like Tom Cruise in *Risky Business*.

Spartacus enters at a normal pace, sniffs the rug, and sits down with a sigh.

I smile and pull out my phone and connect to the cabin's Wi-Fi. Four bars? Full Signal?

*Maybe I underestimated this place.*

There's just one more test. I wander down the short hallway and push open the bathroom door. Tile floor. Folded towels. A shower that looks like it could actually produce hot water. I flush the toilet.

*Strong swirl.*

Then, I turn on the sink to wash my hands.

*No brown water.*

The soap smells faintly of eucalyptus.

*Three for three.*

When I turn to leave, Max is waiting by the door, head tilted, tail giving a slow wag. I reach down and ruffle the hair behind his ears as I pass. "Gonna be a good weekend, boy."

He falls in step behind me as we head back toward the kitchenette, but beats me there. By the time I walk in, he's already sniffing around the fridge. When Crystal sets her purse on the counter, his eyes lift to follow her.

She's smiling in that certain way she does when everything feels right in our world.

"I'll grab the rest of our stuff," I say, moving to the door.

The instant it shuts behind me, high-pitched yelps ring out.

"Be right back!" I call out, which only makes it worse.

At the car, I pop the trunk and stare.

*Yep. Classic me.*

We packed as if we're relocating, not for a weekend trip. And by "we," I obviously mean "me." Dog beds. Bowls. Toys. And then the slippery slope into "just in case" items that would make a doomsday prepper proud. I scan the trunk once more, mentally checking off everything.

A flashlight.

*In case the power goes out.*

Back-up batteries for said flashlight.

*In case the power goes out for the entire weekend.*

Two gallons of water.

*In case the other forty-eight bottles aren't enough.*

Two handguns, safely locked in their cases.

*In case the unthinkable happens.*

I hate that I feel safer knowing the firearms are there. Perhaps some of the paranoia stems from a combination of movies I've seen, like *The Strangers* or *Cabin in the Woods*. Mostly though, I suspect my fear comes from the home invasion attempt that happened over ten years ago at our first apartment in Milledgeville, Georgia. They hadn't gotten in, thank God. But that day is one I still think about when it comes to the safety of those I love.

I exhale, letting the thought fade. Then I notice something that makes me smile. Behind everything is a cooler full of meals and, on top, a foil-covered pan of banana muffins Crystal baked last night. They're the boys' favorite snack. They might be mine too.

I grab the cooler and the pan, along with the food bowls. On the way back, the cooler handle digs into my palm, the bowls *clink* and *clank* together, and I'm doing this weird shuffle-walk toward the cabin. My hand goes numb from the awkward positioning, and I realize I've severely overestimated my carrying capacity. I stop to readjust, setting everything down. When I shake out my fingers, pins and needles prickle up my palm.

As I'm regaining feeling in my hand, I turn just in time to catch the view over the hill. Beyond it, a lake glows under amber skies with the sun hanging above the tree line now. A paddleboat drifts in the distance. A kid cannonballs off a dock. Somewhere across the lake, I hear more splashes, more laughter.

I stand there longer than I mean to, though I couldn't tell you why. Still, a part of me is grateful I stopped.

A bird swoops down in front of me, lands a few feet ahead, then hops along the path before taking off again. I smile, take a deep breath, and keep going.

The boys are waiting on me. And that's reason enough to hurry.

By the time I reach the cabin, Crystal swings the door open before I can knock. Max and Spartacus are right there, tails whipping so hard their bodies look like they might take flight. Max launches at my knees, while Spartacus rises on his hind legs, pawing at my shins.

"Told you I'd be back." I step in, drop the items, and before the door shuts, I do a quick turnaround. "And yes, boys, I'll be back again."

When I finally haul in the last bag, Max is circling my legs so fast I'm dizzy just watching him. Spartacus sits directly on my foot, perhaps to keep me inside with them for good. They're half-barking, half-squealing, fully celebrating my continued existence.

It's a sound I'll never forget.

To them, every return is a miracle.

I laugh, kneeling. Max's tongue swipes across my cheek, and Spartacus head-butts my hand, demanding pets. "I missed you too."

Crystal, the organized one in our tribe, is unpacking the cooler, pulling out the Tupperware containers of food and the bag of treats. She sets the pan of banana muffins on the table, and instantly, both dogs turn in her direction.

They know that pan.

Max stiffens, nose twitching, eyes locked on Crystal.

"Not yet, boy," I tell him.

Crystal peels back the foil an inch. Max springs upward, jaws snapping at air.

"Max!" Crystal quickly turns away. "That's a no-no."

That's our go-to phrase for discipline. It hasn't worked once when food's involved.

Max misses the pan by only inches and lands back on all fours, unfazed, probably calculating his next attempt. Meanwhile, Spartacus sits there watching the scene unfold.

Crystal glances at me, and shakes her head, trying not to laugh. At home when she bakes these muffins, both boys camp out by the oven. Max whines, paces, and generally acts like he's never been fed in his life. Spartacus just sits, occasionally sighing, waiting for the timer to go off.

"All right," Crystal says, reaching for the birthday outfits. "Who's ready?"

Both dogs sprint over.

They don't wear clothes often, just on special occasions and before walks when it's cold outside. To them, I imagine clothes mean something good is about to happen.

Max sits perfectly still while I slide the crimson Alabama shirt over his head. I secure the party hat with the elastic strap under his chin, and he looks up at me with those big dark eyes that seem to say, "I'm doing this for you, you know."

Crystal works on Spartacus across from me, slipping his shirt and hat on. Once his outfit passes her inspection, she reaches for the treat bag. Inside it, she pulls out two, and holds one in each hand, where both dogs can see it. "*Siiit.*"

They sit.

I pull out my phone and snap a dozen photos. Half are blurry; half are perfect. Their photos take up nearly eighty percent of my camera roll. Still, I take a few more because you can never have too many pictures of dogs in Alabama football gear, especially when kickoff against Florida State is tomorrow. Roll Tide!

When I lower my phone, Crystal gives them their prize. Spartacus takes his politely from her hand. Max would gladly take a finger with his snack, so she tosses his onto the ground. This is normal protocol. Before I blink, Max's treat is gone.

Moments later after Spartacus finishes, Crystal's gaze floats from Max, then back to Spartacus. "Who wants Momma Muffins?"

Max curls his tail. Spartacus's ears perk up. Both of them start pacing.

Crystal grabs two muffins. I lift my phone up again, because if I

don't capture this, did it really happen?

She holds the muffins just out of reach.

Their small bodies tremble like two wind-up toys ready to spring loose.

"Happy birthday, boys!"

She sets the muffins down, and Max doesn't even wait for his to touch the floor before he's on it. A wet *gulp* echoes through the cabin, like he's trying to swallow it whole.

For a second, I'm sure he's going to choke. "Slow down!"

*Like that's ever worked.*

He ignores me.

I don't know why I bother. There's no changing him. He is who he is, and that's why we love him.

The muffin disappears in five seconds. Maybe four.

Spartacus picks up his muffin delicately and carries it over to his dog bed. It's a Tempur-Pedic one that matches his coat and that we definitely paid too much for. But they love those beds so much that we bought eight of them—two for each room. Once settled in, muffin between his paws, he begins eating at a pace that can only be described as "mostly civilized."

I'm still recording when Max, having annihilated his own birthday treat, wanders over to inspect his brother's situation.

"Max," I say, lowering the phone. "That's a no-no."

He stops, looks at me, and tilts his head in a way that makes him look like he's genuinely considering my words. Then he looks back at Spartacus. Then at Spartacus's muffin.

I see it. He's plotting. "Maaax."

There's that head-tilt again. The big dark eyes. The slight wag of his tail that says, "Who, me? I'm an angel."

Maybe it was his eyes. Or maybe it was the head-tilt. Either way, the thought hits me: *Seven years old.*

My chest tightens.

*Forty-nine in human years. Older than me.*

I turn away before Crystal can see, pretending to scroll on my phone. A lump forms in my throat. The screen goes hazy.

Most small dogs live twelve to fourteen years. I know this. I've Googled it eight hundred times, usually at 2:00 a.m. when my brain decides it's a great time to catastrophize everything.

*Seven means we're past the halfway point.*

My heart is pounding now. I can hear it.

*Seven means maybe—maybe—five years left. If we're lucky.*

I need to sit down, but I can't.

*Five more birthdays. Five more Christmases. Five more years to hear the sound of little paws pattering around the house. Five years isn't enough. Neither would fifty.*

I know this is what I signed up for. Everyone who gets a dog knows this. But standing here in this cabin, it feels cruel, this bargain we make for love.

A wet nose nudges my ankle.

When I look down, Max is staring up at me as if I'm the greatest thing that's ever happened to him. As if these years together have been the best years imaginable, and he has zero regrets about any of it—including the time he snatched an entire pumpkin pie off the counter and left the rest of us without Thanksgiving dessert.

I crouch, and he puts his paws on my knee, stretching up to lick my chin.

"Hey, boy." My voice comes out quieter than I intended.

If he only knew that I feel the same about *him*. And that I'd give anything for more time.

Behind me, Crystal murmurs something to Spartacus.

Max licks my face again. I scratch behind his ears, and he leans into it, eyes closing. He's not thinking about five years down the road.

He's only thinking about right now. This moment. This person in front of him. This cabin. This lake. This summer evening, when the light is perfect and there are still muffin crumbs on his chin.

My mind drifts, replaying it all: Every stolen sandwich. Every time he's made me laugh when I wanted to cry. Every truth he's taught me about life just by being exactly who he is. I smile through the sting in my eyes.

I don't want this to end.

But one day it will.

Time will run out.

Though when it does, I hope my heart remembers that the love never will.

I wipe my eyes with my shirt and look at Max. He's *still* here. Still mine to hold, to laugh with, and to love. And for now, that'll be enough.

Seven years ago, by some small miracle of timing or fate, a little black dog came into my life and somehow, he made it bigger ...

*"In the back seat, two pairs of eyes track our every move."*

*"Just feed us already!"*

*"It's all about US today!"*

*"Not getting up unless I get a snack."*

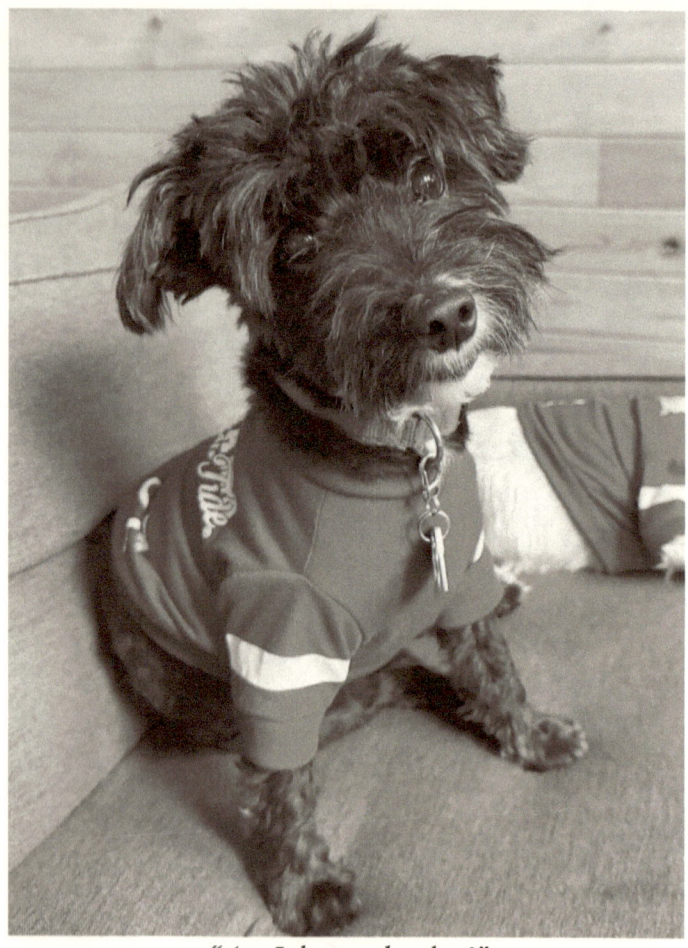

*"Am I the cute brother?"*

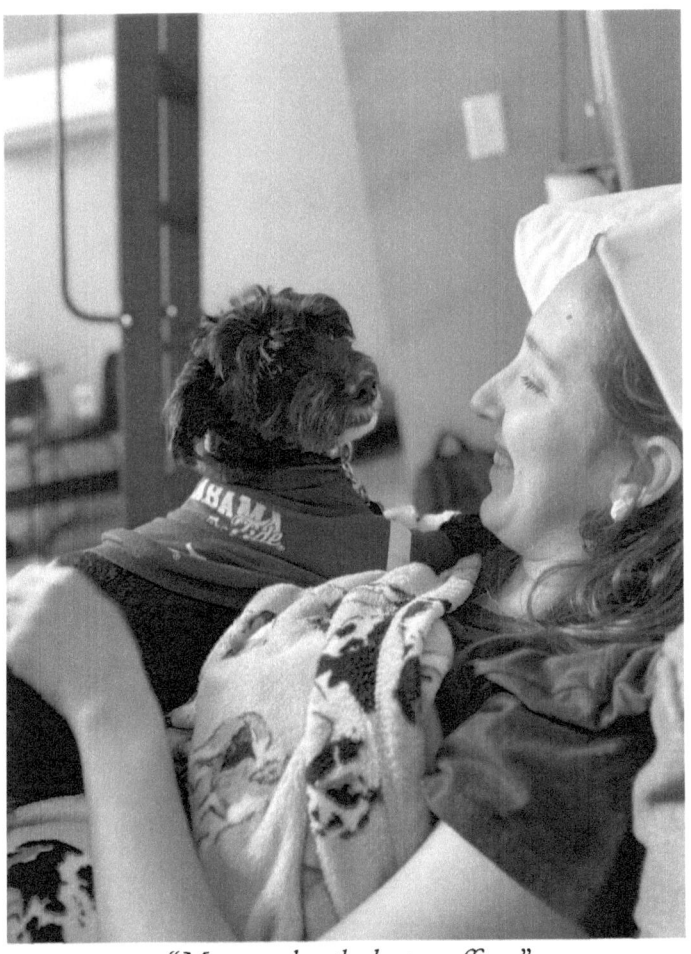

*"Mom makes the best muffins."*

# 2

# Blaze

**Year One**

## 2018

"LET'S GET A DOG."

The words slipped out before I even realized I meant them.

Crystal had been campaigning since 2013, spamming texts to my phone with adorable puppy photos. I held out for five years until one September night, sitting side by side with our headsets on, mid-game, when I finally took mine off and said the words she'd been waiting for.

I couldn't tell you what changed. I wasn't any more "ready" that night than I'd been those years before. But maybe that's the point.

We spend so much of life waiting to feel ready for the big, scary things we want. We convince ourselves that we're lacking the talent, resources, or the time. Maybe even all three. Sometimes, though, you just have to decide you're willing to figure it out as you go.

Two weeks later, we were standing in a Chick-fil-A parking lot.

"This here's Blaze," the lady said, holding him out.

*Blaze.*

Crystal and I had already decided we were changing his name, but I wasn't about to tell her that while she was holding our new dog.

We had chosen to rename him Maximus—well, mostly me—thanks to my lifelong obsession with *Gladiator*. In middle school, I'd seen it at the theater and was captivated by Russell Crowe's character, Maximus. Years later, I even got a full sleeve tattoo inspired by the film. So when it came time to name our dog, there was really only one choice.

When I took Max from her, he was lighter than I expected. And I had to hold my breath.

*Stinkimus?*

He smelled like he'd smoked every cigarette she'd ever lit in that Jeep, then rolled in the ashtray for good measure. The stench brought me right back to high school. Not because I was a smoker, but because I'd tried to be one, exactly once.

My friend and I had snuck out to the tennis courts one night, and in a stroke of pure teenage stupidity, I shoved an entire pack of cigarettes in my mouth and lit them all. I don't know what I expected to happen, but I coughed so hard that they went flying everywhere. I stomped them all out and decided it wasn't as cool as I had imagined. I haven't touched a cigarette since.

Before I could stop myself, I'd already made the mistake of mentioning a bath, which apparently the lady had *just* given him. The death stare she gave me suggested we wrap this transaction up quickly.

Crystal handed over the cash, I mumbled something about needing to get going, and we made our quick getaway with our new family member.

Now, I need to address something.

Maximus wasn't a rescue. We bought him from a breeder, and I'm not going to pretend otherwise. At this time in my life, I didn't understand the scope of animal suffering and homelessness that exists because of backyard breeding. I just didn't know. And while I'll be adopting from shelters in the future, I could never regret Max.

Some readers even stopped reading my first book, *Pawprints on Our Hearts,* the moment they learned we'd bought a dog from a breeder.

I get it. I really do.

People care deeply about this, and for good reason. If there's one thing I've learned in the thirty-eight years of my existence, it's that we're at our best as humans when we educate each other, not cancel one another for things we've done, especially when we didn't know any better.

But I'm also not here to judge anyone else's choices. There's nothing I can do or say that will change someone's mind if they're not ready to hear it.

Think about it.

Has a single argument on Facebook ever changed anyone's mind? Has shaming a stranger in a comment section ever resulted in them saying, "You know what, you're absolutely right. I'm completely changing my worldview because of your reply"?

Of course not.

So for the record, I'm not here to change anyone. I'm just here to love—and at the end of my days, I hope that'll be enough.

The first thing we did when we arrived home that afternoon was give Max a bath.

I filled the kitchen sink with warm water while Crystal held him, testing the temperature with my hand. The moment he realized what was coming, his whole body tensed.

"It's okay, boy," I said, taking him from her.

When I lowered him into the water slowly, he didn't fight at all. Crystal squeezed dog shampoo into her palm and started working it into his coat, and I grabbed the sprayer and started rinsing. The water turned a grayish color that I'm pretty sure shouldn't exist.

*Ehhh.*

After Crystal lifted him out of the sink, water dripped from his hair onto the counter. She set him gently on the kitchen floor and reached for a towel. "Hold still," she said, drying him as she laughed. He tolerated it for a beat before he squirmed against her hands like he'd had enough of this spa treatment.

When she finally pulled the towel away, he tore through the kitchen, darting between our legs, and raced into the living room. He looped around the couch, slid across the rug, and came barreling back toward us, eyes bright and wild.

We just stood there laughing, watching him zoom from room to room, burning off whatever energy that tiny body could hold.

And somewhere between the sound of his paws and the trail of wet footprints across the floor, I realized something that probably should've occurred to me before we drove to a Chick-fil-A parking lot to buy a dog from a stranger.

*We're parents now.*

Dog parents, sure. But parents.

Crystal and I had talked about kids before. But after our less than desirable childhoods and relationships with our parents, we'd realized that we only liked the *idea* of having children. What we liked more, though, were naps, spontaneous trips, and saving money. A dog felt like the right compromise. All the love, less responsibility, and we could still sleep in.

At least that's what we'd told ourselves.

For the rest of that afternoon and into the evening, we watched Maximus play with his new toy. Crystal had bought him a rubber ring with a rope attached—one of those indestructible-looking things the package promised would last forever.

It took him about fifteen minutes to prove that was a lie.

The rope tore off, so we tossed it in the trash. But the ring itself seemed sturdy enough, and he carried it around proudly like he'd bought it himself.

I got down on the floor with him and grabbed one end of the ring. He immediately clamped down on the other side with his tiny teeth and pulled back. I gave it a gentle tug.

The sound that came out of him surprised me. It was a low, ferocious growl. Primal even, like he was channeling his inner ancient wolf. Somehow, this little ball of fluff was making a noise that belonged to a dog ten times his size. He looked up at me, still gripping the toy—with a Denzel Washington in *Training Day* type of energy—as if declaring, "I run this house now. You just live here."

We played tug of war for another few minutes, and every time I pulled, he'd let out that same ridiculous growl. It would've been more intimidating if it weren't so absurdly adorable.

After Max had gotten bored with the game and abandoned his toy, Crystal grabbed her selfie stick and iPhone and crouched down to film at his eye level.

"Max-i-mus," she said in that high-pitched baby-talk voice people use with puppies, "you gonna get me? Huh? You gonna catch me?"

His ears perked up.

She took off.

The moment he saw her move, he chased after her, his little legs moving so fast they barely seemed to touch the ground. He was locked in on that phone at the end of the selfie stick, nipping at it every time he got close enough.

I sat on the couch, watching them go through the living room and down the hallway. When they rounded the corner at the kitchen island, his legs went out from under him on the laminate, all four paws scrambling for traction like a cartoon character. He slid a few inches, regained his footing, and took off again at full speed.

Crystal laughed—really laughed—and kept filming, looking back at him over her shoulder, saying things like, "Come on, Max! Come get me!"

I'd never seen Crystal like this. There was a lightness on her face I hadn't seen since ... I don't know. Maybe ever. But this was her as a dog mom. And Maximus, this tiny creature who'd only been in our lives for a few hours, was already so sure of where he belonged.

There's something about witnessing pure joy that leaves you somewhere between awe and gratitude.

It struck me then that in our attempts to create a comfortable life, we'd traded late-night hangouts for overtime. Weekend spontaneity had become recovery days. And those days eventually went away and turned into more grinding. Even the moments between us felt scheduled. We'd become productive and responsible. We'd become adults who took ourselves too seriously.

Maybe that's why Maximus came into our lives—to remind us we'd spent so long building a life, we'd forgotten to *live* it.

The thought lingered until Max eventually wore himself out and plopped onto the floor, panting. We decided to call it a night and took him out in the backyard for one last bathroom break. When his paws touched the grass, he exploded across the yard, darting in circles around the fence line. Every few seconds, he'd look back at us, freeze, then bolt in the opposite direction.

"Maximus! Come here, boy," Crystal called, crouching down.

He ran straight toward her, then veered off at the last second, completing another lap.

She glanced at me. "Did he pee?"

I smiled. "Nope."

*Blaze. Yeah, makes sense now.*

By the time we finally coaxed him inside—treats may have been involved—he was panting hard, tongue lolling out. We led him to his crate in the kitchen, and I kneeled to refold the blanket, tucking it neatly into each corner before he climbed in. We dimmed the lights and made our way down the hall.

Crystal and I crawled into bed, exhausted but excited. We talked about all the places we'd take Max: the park, the beach, and every dog-friendly coffee shop we could find. And instead of sleeping, we spent the next hour scrolling through photos and videos of Max from earlier.

"Look at this one," Crystal said, showing me a shot of him sitting contentedly.

She opened Facebook and stared at the photo, smiling to herself. Her thumbs hovered before she typed, deleted, and typed again. Finally, she'd settled on something and hit post.

I pulled out my phone and went to her page. Within seconds, there were eighty-seven likes, then ninety. A dozen comments followed, all some version of *He's so cute!* or *Adorable!*

Crystal gave a sleepy sigh, setting her phone on the nightstand. I did the same, and for the first time all night, the house felt still.

A minute later, so did we.

That first night, we learned two important things about our new roommate.

Thing one: Max hated sleeping alone in the kitchen.

Around midnight, it started. Whimpering, then crying, then full-on howling like he'd never see us again. The parenting instinct we gained from every training video we'd absorbed in the days leading up to that night, advised us to ignore his behavior in situations like this. We were determined to "raise him right."

Though it was difficult, we followed the advice. Mostly.

Thing two: Appeasement works.

At 3:00 a.m., howling echoed through the house. I stumbled out of bed in my boxers, opened his kennel, and carried him to the backyard. The September air hit me, still warm but carrying the first hint of fall. I set Max down on the grass, and he started sniffing around.

I waited, arms crossed, and looked up.

Thin clouds drifted across the sky, breaking just enough for a few stars to peek through. Even as a kid, I always felt something when I looked up at the stars. Not a religious something exactly, though maybe that's part of it. More like ... connected to God in a way that makes you feel small and grateful all at once.

Standing there in my backyard, groggy and barefoot, I felt it again. That sense that I was exactly where I was supposed to be, doing exactly what I was supposed to be doing, even if I had no idea what that might be.

The sound of rustling grass pulled me back. I turned and saw Max a few feet away, still searching for the exact right spot in the entire galaxy to pee. Seconds later, he lifted his leg and did the deed.

*Mission accomplished.*

"Good boy," I mumbled, as he trotted back toward me. I bent down, scooped him up, and he licked my chin. I couldn't help but smile.

Back inside, I placed him in his crate. He looked up at me with those dark eyes, then a whine followed.

"Shhh, your momma's sleeping," I whispered, sliding a few of his treats through the kennel bars. He took them, tail wagging.

I waited a minute.

*That was easy.*

Then a bark. Then two. Then three.

I tried another treat. And another. Pretty soon, I was basically paying him in snacks to go to sleep.

I made it only halfway down the hall before the crying started again. I turned around, went back to the kitchen, crouched by the crate, and whispered a few comforting words I'm sure he didn't understand, and walked away.

Silence.

*Maybe this is it. Maybe he'll actually—*

Then came the whimpering, sharper this time.

I looked back, and he was still staring at me. Every article I'd read said not to give in, but those people had clearly never met Maximus.

A paw scraped the inside of the crate, then another, until the metal rattled like he was digging a tunnel to freedom or auditioning for a patty-cake championship.

*Yorkipoo or wolverine?*

I sighed, went back, and unlatched the crate. The moment I opened the door, he climbed into my arms and buried his face against my neck. His little body trembled, and I could feel his heartbeat thudding against my chest.

Going back to bed didn't feel right—not with him shaking like that—so I headed for the couch. I sat down, settling him on my lap. He looked up at me with those dark eyes. I rubbed his head in circles, then worked my way down his back, through his soft hair. His breathing slowed. I kept going with gentle strokes along his sides and back up to his ears. Gradually, his body softened against me, and his eyes fluttered shut.

For another minute, I waited, making sure he was really out, then carefully stood up. He stayed limp in my arms as I walked slowly back to the kitchen, placed him gently in his crate on top of the blanket, and latched the door shut as quietly as I could.

I held my breath, backing away one step at a time. Before I knew it, I'd made it all the way to the bedroom and back into bed. I don't even remember falling asleep. And though I didn't know it then, someday I'd look back on this night and realize it wasn't just the start of his life with us. It was the moment ours began again, too.

But I'm getting ahead of myself.

First, there was the sandwich incident.

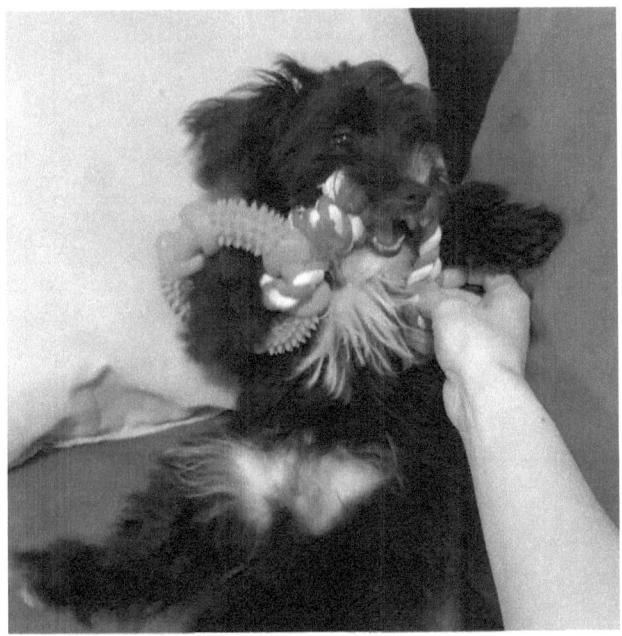

*"Thanks for my new toy. About to destroy it!"*

*"I look innocent, don't I?"*

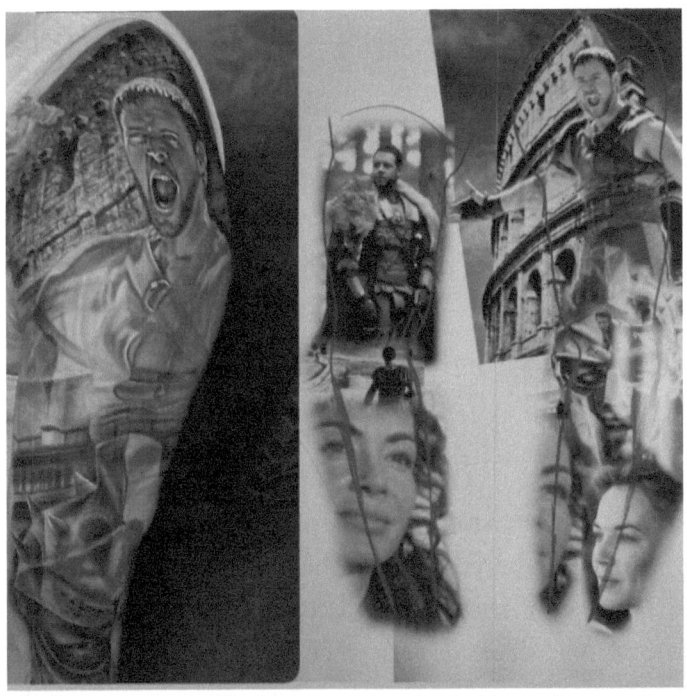

*Progress on my Gladiator tattoo sleeve. I've only seen the
movie fifty-ish times. Tattoo done by Robert Madera in
Savannah, Georgia. Instagram: @robertmadera*

# 3

# Art of a Heist

My alarm blared. I shot upright.

Sunlight filtered through the blinds—too much of it.

I threw off the covers and scrambled to the laundry room. The dryer door screeched open, and I grabbed my button-up shirt and pants. They clung to my hands.

*Great.*

I hadn't started it last night.

Standing there, I weighed my options. As an executive director at Chick-fil-A, being late wasn't an option. My team counted on me to set the tone, and October was one of our busiest months, which meant all hands on deck. But showing up on time in wet clothes wasn't the image—or the feeling—I wanted for a twelve-hour day. This time, I hit the dryer button and started what would become the longest twenty minutes of my morning.

*Maybe I can still make it.*

While I waited, I figured I'd at least make breakfast. My stomach growled. I hadn't eaten since yesterday's lunch. When I had finally remembered, I was already in bed and was more tired than hungry. Between work and Max, I'd somehow forgotten to feed myself.

I headed to the pantry, scanning for something quick. A near-empty bag of Cap'n Crunch caught my eye. I poured what was left into a bowl and opened the fridge. No milk.

*Hmmm.*

Water was doable; I'd done it before. Not great, but passable. I'd tried orange juice once. That mistake didn't need repeating.

*Eat it dry maybe?*

If I was going to eat something dry, I might as well find something better. So, I set the bowl aside and checked the pantry for ramen noodles. My usual stash was gone.

*Figures.*

Then I spotted it.

Old Faithful, right where it always was: peanut butter. Not the crunchy kind I usually buy. The store had been out, so creamy it was. I'd survive.

I gazed at it, wondering whether creamy even counted as real peanut butter, then decided now wasn't the time for a Socratic debate. So I grabbed the jar, pulled out bread, and started assembling a sandwich at the kitchen counter. I glanced toward the living room. Max lay on his back, legs in the air, completely unmoved by my breakfast crisis.

The phone rang. The name flashing across it made my stomach tighten.

*Why's he calling this early?*

The last time he'd called this early, a delivery truck hadn't shown, the drive-thru was packed with angry customers, and I'd spent my day off cleaning up that mess.

I sighed, then swiped to answer. I wedged the phone between shoulder and ear, still spreading peanut butter.

"Are you at the store?" my boss asked.

*What now?*

I glanced at the microwave clock. "No, but I'm heading out."

"Good. Listen, are we delivering twenty or thirty nugget trays for the event?"

My phone buzzed against my ear; I grabbed it and glanced down.

It was a text from my kitchen manager:

> **Walk-in cooler's down.**

*Of course.*

I readjusted the phone. "Sorry, what was that?"

"The catering order—how many trays?"

"Uh ... I can't remember off the top of my head, but I can—"

Another buzz:

> **Eddie called out.**

*Today's my day.*

Silence on the other end. "All right. I'll be there in fifteen. I'll check it myself."

"Yes, sir. See you soon." I hung up.

*Gotta hurry.*

I exhaled, grateful it hadn't been worse. Then I dropped the knife in the sink, shoved the bread and peanut butter away, and wiped the counter in one motion. I threw on my still-damp clothes, fixed my hair, and tried to remember where I'd left my keys. Crystal would've known—she always did—but she was already at work. I checked the counter, the coffee table, even the dryer. Nothing.

By the time I found them, buried under a month-old pile of mail, I'd almost forgotten the sandwich. I grabbed my wallet, keys, and walked back to the counter to finish what I'd started.

*What in the—*

I stood there, blinking at the empty space.

*No sandwich.*

For a second, I thought maybe I'd never made it. Maybe I'd imagined the whole thing in my sleep-deprived haze.

I turned, and there he was, sitting on the couch, peanut butter smeared across his snout. Max looked at me with those dark, innocent eyes that seemed to say, "It wasn't me."

"Max!"

His tail wagged.

"That's a no-no."

Another wag. More enthusiastic this time.

I should've been mad and put him in time-out or something. But I was too hungry and too late to care. I just needed food and to get out the door.

*Now.*

I grabbed another plate and moved to the pantry. The peanut butter was back in its usual spot, right where I'd actually put it away for once—same with the knife and bread. Of course, the one time I listen to Crystal and clean up after myself, it costs me thirty seconds I didn't have.

I spread the peanut butter faster this time and slapped the sandwich together, then grabbed my keys, my bag, and headed for the door. I barely made it three steps before—

A blur of black hair launched off the couch.

He hit the ground running.

Leaped. Perfect form.

The sandwich—snatched clean out of my hand.

For a second, I stood there, hand frozen in midair where the sandwich used to be.

Then my brain caught up.

"Max!"

He was already gone, tearing through the living room with my breakfast clenched between his teeth. I dropped my stuff and went after him.

Max jumped onto the couch, bounced off, darted under the coffee table, and came out the other side before I'd even made it halfway across the room.

I lunged for him.

Missed.

He looped around the kitchen island. I followed, nearly slipping on the tile. By the time I recovered, he was already back in the living room, sitting under the table with a piece of the sandwich still intact.

"Give it back," I said, breathing hard, pointing at him like that would somehow work.

He tilted his head.

"That's a no-no!"

He took a bite.

I crawled under the table.

He darted out the other side.

I got up, and he was already three moves ahead, weaving between the couch cushions.

My breath came quicker now. Not gasping, but enough to remind me I hadn't done real cardio in years.

Max sat a few feet away with the last corner of my sandwich dangling from his mouth. He gave it one final chew, swallowed, and licked his paws like nothing had happened at all.

I checked my phone.

*Really late.*

I could make a third sandwich. Surely he couldn't pull that off again. But I was already too far behind. So I grabbed my keys, my bag, and headed out the door—sandwichless.

In the car, I tossed my bag onto the passenger seat and started the engine. The dashboard clock reminded me I was further behind than I'd planned to be. My stomach growled. For a moment, I just sat there. Then I smiled.

This was my life now—one where a tiny dog could outsmart me, outrun me, and steal my breakfast twice in ten minutes ... all while I went to work to buy more food and pay for the roof over his head so he could try it again tomorrow.

Still, I didn't hate it. Max was ours, and we were his. Even if that meant going to work hungry every once in a while.

After the sandwich incident, we got more careful. We stopped leaving food unattended and started putting things higher, farther back out of his reach. We thought we'd finally figured him out.

By Thanksgiving, Max had adapted.

We spent the first part of the week at my parents' place in south Atlanta, visiting my old dog, Lexi—fourteen now, but still hanging on. It was the first time she and Max had met, and watching them together did something to me I didn't have words for. I would've stayed longer for Lexi, but a few days around the "family" was plenty. We headed home early to do our own Thanksgiving.

Back in Hinesville, Georgia, we kept it simple. Crystal and I brought home a chicken-strip tray from work. It seemed easier than cooking a whole turkey and, honestly, just as good. Still, Crystal spent the morning making her mashed potatoes and gravy from scratch and a pan of sweet potatoes. The croissants were store-bought; even so, severely underrated. And she'd picked up a bakery pumpkin pie that came with its own tub of whipped cream.

We loaded our plates, settled in for football, and I thought this could be the best Thanksgiving meal we'd ever had.

Max had already gotten his Thanksgiving treat—a small plate of sweet potatoes he'd inhaled in seconds. But apparently, that wasn't enough. He appeared at my knee, staring up at me with those big dark eyes. If Max had taught me anything, it was that no creature lied better than a dog who'd already eaten.

"Max, you just had a whole plate."

He tilted his head.

I broke off a piece of croissant and tossed it his way. He caught it midair, swallowed it whole, then returned to his post by my leg.

"Seriously?"

Another tilt—this time with a small whine for effect.

I broke off another piece. Then another. Each time, I told myself it was the last, until I looked down at my plate. Only one of the three croissants I'd started with remained, and even that one was pretty much gone.

Crystal glanced over and laughed. "Did you just give him your entire roll?"

"No."

*Technically true.*

"Almost three."

She shook her head. "No, no, Max. Stop begging your daddy."

Max looked at her, sighed, and trotted back to his bed in the corner.

Ten minutes into the game, I heard it.

A heavy thud.

Then, the unmistakable sound of—

I turned just in time to see Max freeze mid-chew, pumpkin pie covering his snout. He looked up, paused for half a second, then doubled down on his mission.

"Max!"

We both bolted for the kitchen. Crystal beat me there and scooped him up. He looked at us with pure joy in his eyes, tail wagging, and completely unrepentant.

I stared at the mess. "How'd he even—we pushed everything to the back."

Crystal set Max down and shooed him out of the kitchen. "Go. You're a naughty boy."

He gave us one last look, tongue dangling, before sauntering back into the living room.

"Let's find out." Crystal pulled out her phone, opened the camera app, and held it between us. She rewound the footage.

*There he goes.*

Max had jumped up, grabbed the corner of the towel the pie sat on, and yanked the whole thing down.

I shouldn't have been surprised. For a dog his size, Max had serious leg muscles—glutes you could bounce a quarter off. Probably from all that couch-to-couch leaping or secret squats while we were at work.

*Gluteus Maximus?*

On the screen, he made his next move. The pie had landed upside down, splattered across the floor. That hadn't slowed him at all. He'd gone at it as if he'd been waiting his entire life for this moment.

Crystal looked at me. "We've created a monster."

I studied the carnage, trying to decide what disaster it resembled most. Mount Vesuvius? Chernobyl? I'd been thinking about that pie all day. From the time I woke up, through that meal, and through the first few minutes of the game. I'd earned that pie. We both had.

"Hold on," I said.

Crystal looked at me. "Kerk. No."

"Might be salvageable."

"Kerk."

"Just let me look."

I hated wasting food. Especially food we paid for. Running low food costs—at work and at home—was equally important.

I crouched to inspect the mess. Pumpkin filling smeared across the tile, crust shards, nose prints stamped in orange, and a tin pan bent at an angle. Most of it was clearly ruined. But there on the far side, a section looked almost untouched.

*Maybe.*

I grabbed a fork.

"Don't do it."

"This part's fine," I said, gently prying at it.

"His tongue was literally on that."

"Not here."

"I can just grab another tomorrow when the store opens."

"Tomorrow's too far away." I managed to dig out a piece about the size of a saltine cracker. Maybe smaller. I held it up. "See?"

I popped it in my mouth.

*Pretty good.*

"You really just did that."

"What? It's fine."

She raised an eyebrow and turned toward the cabinet. "I'll get the towels and spray."

"Hold on—might be another good piece here."

"Well, hurry up."

As she walked away, I glanced at the living room. Max sat at the edge of the kitchen, head tilted, watching me with what could only be described as a grin.

Little did I know then, throughout the years he'd steal many more meals. His biggest heist would be a six-inch Publix sub. Then there was the time he snatched an entire slice of pizza from a friend's plate when they came over for a movie night. And I can't forget about the bowl of chili I left on the coffee table when I went to answer the door. It was gone in the twenty seconds it took me to sign for a package. I'm sure there will be plenty more heists in the future.

Watching him that night, pumpkin pie still smeared across his snout, I realized Max didn't just love food. He was devoted to it. He planned, waited, and positioned himself for every chance that came his way. He never gave up and never doubted that the next meal was worth the effort.

Most of my life, I've doubted myself. I've wondered if the dreams I had were even possible. I've fallen on my face more times than I can count, collected more second-place medals than I care to admit, and learned to expect *almost but not quite.*

Max never seemed to second-guess anything. He just acted, certain the world would provide what he needed, when he needed it.

I like to think he loves me as much as he loves food. Though, judging by that pie, I'm probably second place—again.

*Too soon?*

Still, I'm grateful. Because of him, a lot of things feel a little more possible.

*"I'm not looking at your plate."*

*"Call me Gluteus Maximus."*

*"Look into my dark eyes ... Now, give me your pie!"*

# 4

# The Max Tax

By December, Maximus had mastered potty training. Accidents were a rarity. Even in those first few weeks after we'd brought him home, he'd learned to approach the back door when he needed to go. Still, we wanted an easier way for him to tell us—something that didn't require us keeping an eye on him 24/7. So, we got him some of those doggy bells that hang from the back door handle.

Every time he went to the door, we'd gently take his paw and tap it against the bells before letting him outside. At first, he'd look at us confused, as if to say, "What are you people doing with my paw?" But within a week, he'd figured it out. He'd also figured out something else: the bells didn't just mean "I need to pee." They meant "door opens," and to him, an open door meant *possibility*.

Our days started going like this:

*Ring-Ring-Ring.*

"Good boy!"

He'd dart outside, do a lap around the yard, sniff every bush and blade of grass, and come back inside.

Five minutes later:

*Ring-Ring-Ring.*

"Again?"

Another lap, more sniffing, and zero bathroom activity.

We caught on pretty quickly. But what were we supposed to do? Ignore him and risk him having an accident inside? We'd worked too hard on the potty training to backtrack now. So, we let him out every single time and hoped for the best.

Max had learned we'd always get up and open the door for him. And of course, he learned to take advantage of that.

I squirted lighter fluid onto the charcoal for the fourth time and stepped back, waiting for the flames to settle. Behind me, the door opened.

In the yard, Max was tearing from one corner of the fence to the other, then taking off again like he was training for the Olympics.

"How's it going?" Crystal called out.

I coughed. "Great," I said, waving through a cloud of smoke. For my first time grilling, the Burger King commercials had definitely oversold the experience.

"Max still out here?"

Smoke billowed around my face. I coughed again, then turned toward her and pointed with the spatula. "Yeah. There he goes again."

She smiled, closed the door, and disappeared inside.

*Really?*

I'd expected some kind of backup here. Instead, it felt like she'd caught the last chopper out of 'Nam and left me to fight this thing alone.

Twenty minutes later, I was still hunched over the grill, spatula in hand, trying to pry the first burger off the grate. It wouldn't budge. I wedged the spatula under it and pushed. The patty tore in half.

"Come on."

By the time I finally got two intact burgers onto the plate—only slightly charred, mostly edible—my forearm ached and I smelled like a campfire. I opened the back door. "Max! Come on, boy!"

He trotted in, tongue lolling out, and headed straight for his water bowl.

By the counter, Crystal was waiting with buns, lettuce, tomato, and cheese. "Took you long enough," she said, grinning.

I smirked. "Discount grill. Not completely my fault."

We built our burgers together, grabbed some chips and drinks, then headed to the couch. She hit play to start our Christmas movie marathon. For about thirty seconds, everything was perfect. Then—

*Ring-Ring-Ring.*

"Your turn," Crystal said, not looking away from the TV.

"I got the last one."

"And I got the two before that."

We played this game every time, while Max sat by the door, waiting for one of us to cave.

*Ring-Ring-Ring. Ring-Ring-Ring.*

"Okay, okay." I set my plate on the coffee table and stood. "Come on, boy." I headed over and opened the door.

Max didn't move.

*What?*

He glimpsed outside, looked up at me, then scanned the living room.

He bolted.

But not outside.

He shot past my legs, through the kitchen, and launched himself toward the coffee table.

I sprang forward, chasing after him. "Max!"

He went airborne like a little missile.

Crystal lunged, arms outstretched. Missed.

Mid-air, his jaws clamped down on something from my plate.

I stopped at the table, and Max was already at the hallway, scarfing down whatever it was.

I looked down at my food.

The top bun of my burger was gone.

Crystal and I looked at each other. Then at the empty spot on my burger where my bun used to be. Then back to each other. A few seconds later—

*Ring-Ring-Ring.*

And there he was—at the back door *again*. Our boy was both a con man and a genius.

As I stood there, bun-less, I replayed what had just happened in my head, breaking down his methodology:

- Step One: Ring bells.

- Step Two: Wait for human to stand.

- Step Three: When said human opens door, ignore door entirely.

- Step Four: Sprint to unguarded food.

- Step Five: Snatch, run, and devour as quickly as possible.

- Bonus Step: If caught, deploy the adorable "puppy dog eyes" to avoid all consequences.

It was foolproof, repeatable, and—given a few refinements—scalable, even. He could've sold this system to other dogs on a late-night infomercial.

I could practically hear the voice-over: "Are *you* tired of watching your humans eat all the good food? Call now and learn Max's Five-Step Food Acquisition System! But wait—there's more. If you buy today, we'll include one bonus step that'll change your life forever, your satisfaction guaranteed or your money back."

From then on, we learned to bring our plates with us whenever Max rang the bells, but in our hearts, we accepted that sometimes, we'd just have to pay the Max Tax.

I walked over and opened the back door. This time, Max actually went outside.

Of course he did. He'd already gotten what he wanted. For now.

I headed to the kitchen and grabbed another bun from the bag, reassembling my burger while keeping one eye on the door. A minute later, Max trotted back in, tail wagging like he'd done nothing wrong.

I smiled because, as annoying as it was to lose a part of my lunch to a tiny con artist, there was something strangely impressive about watching him work.

Max knew exactly what he was doing. And if he could talk, I'm pretty sure he'd look me dead in the eye and say, "Don't hate the player, hate the game."

*"Must ... have ... human food!"*

*"Nothing to see here folks. Definitely not searching for snacks."*

# 5

# Double or Nothing

"Ready ... Go!"

The tennis ball sailed across the yard, arcing high before disappearing into the afternoon sun. Maximus tore after it, ears flapping, and back legs kicking up dirt.

"Good boy!" I called, though he didn't need the encouragement. He was already halfway back, panting, and clearly expecting round two.

I threw again. And again. And again. Somewhere around the tenth toss, my shoulder started to throb. I dropped my arm and shook it out, trying to remember if I'd ever had to stretch before playing fetch.

*Probably not.*

By the twentieth throw, I was done.

Inside, I leaned against the fridge, gulping water and wondering how professional pitchers survived a season of this. A moment later, I heard the jingle of his tags.

Max sauntered in, tennis ball in his mouth before dropping it at my feet.

I stared down at him, shaking my head. "Daddy's tired."

His tail wagged faster.

That dog could keep going and going. No matter what time of day it was, he was always down to play. I was still relatively young at thirty-one, but sometimes I felt bad that I couldn't keep up with him. Then again, I didn't know anyone who really could or would be crazy enough to try.

The truth was, his energy needed an outlet we couldn't always give him.

Crystal and I both had jobs that required us to be gone for nine, sometimes twelve hours a day. During that time, Max stayed in his kennel. Every day, at least one of us would slip home during our lunch break—fifteen minutes, maybe twenty if we were lucky—to let him out.

He'd burst from the kennel the second we opened it, race circles around the living room, and grab his toy. We'd take him outside, play for a few minutes, give him fresh water, and then came the hard part: "Come on, Max. Back in."

He'd look at us like we were Brutus and the rest of the Roman Senate. "Et tu, Mom and Dad?"

But back in the kennel he went.

When we'd finally come home for the night, he'd shoot out of it, bouncing off furniture, skidding across the floor, leaping from couch to chair and then doing it all over again. His joy seemed bigger than the space he had to live it in.

I smiled watching him, but something about it pained me. All that joy, all that life—and most of his day was spent in a kennel waiting for us to come home.

That wasn't a life. Max deserved better.

I rolled onto my side for what had to be the hundredth time, bunching the pillow under my arm and flipping it to the cool side before kicking one leg out from under the sheet.

Nothing helped.

The clock on my nightstand read *11:37 p.m.* Not terribly late, but late for us, considering the alarm would go off at six.

I rubbed my eyes and did what any responsible adult does when they can't sleep: grab their phone. Within seconds, I was scrolling through memes, headlines, and Googling random things like, *Can a snake bite you while you're on the toilet?* and *How tall was Jesus Christ?*

After a short but surprisingly deep dive into the underbelly of Reddit, a Facebook video caught my attention—a dog pacing in a shelter kennel. Two steps forward. Turn. Two steps back. Over and over.

I sighed and locked my screen. The bluish glow from my phone faded from the room as I stared at the ceiling.

"You awake?"

Crystal rolled over. "Yeah."

"I've been thinking."

"About?"

"Max. I don't think we should keep him in the kennel all day anymore."

She was quiet for a second. "I've been thinking the same thing."

The next morning, we set up a small area between the kitchen and the garage using a baby gate. It wasn't much—about the size of a walk-in closet—but to Max, it might as well have been a football field. He circled the space a few times, as if testing whether it was really all his.

When I kneeled to check the gate, he looked up at me with bright eyes. Then he stretched, yawned, and plopped down with a satisfied huff. He seemed happier—or maybe just confused by his suddenly bigger world. Either way, it felt like the right call.

I crouched beside him and scratched his head. "We'll be back soon, okay?"

His ears perked as if he believed every word.

My knees cracked as I stood, and as we left for work, I looked back one last time. He was still there, head tilted, watching us go.

"This is good," Crystal said. "He'll be fine."

I nodded and locked the door behind us, thinking we were geniuses.

Later that morning, we arrived home. The second Crystal opened the door, an ammonia-like smell hit, stinging my eyes.

She stepped inside and stopped. "Oh, no."

I followed closely behind. Then I saw it—everywhere.

Pee puddles floated on the laminate floor. It looked less like an accident and more like Max had attempted to create a new Great Lake.

*Lake Pissimus.*

In the corner, sat a towering pile I didn't need to approach to identify.

*Mount Dookimus.*

"What the—" Crystal moved past me, staring at the floor. "Max has never done this."

He hadn't. Not once since those first few days. But that wasn't even the worst part.

"Crystal."

"What?"

I pointed at the floor near the baby gate.

The laminate was peeled up in strips, chewed and torn away. I crouched down and touched the edge. Underneath, I could see the concrete foundation.

"He chewed right through it," I said.

Crystal bent down beside me, running her hand over the damage. "How's that even possible?"

I didn't have an answer. We'd only been gone for a few hours.

Max ambled over and licked my hand, then Crystal's, like everything was perfect again now that we were home.

I wanted to be mad. But looking at him, I just felt helpless.

We cleaned it up, scrubbed the floors, told ourselves it was a fluke, and went back to work.

*He'll adjust.*

The next day, there was even more pee and more destruction.

*Maybe not.*

By the end of week one, the baseboards were chewed to splinters. Two weeks in, that room looked like a demolition site. He'd done at least a couple grand worth of damage.

"This can't keep happening," I said one night, holding a trash bag full of chewed-up laminate.

Crystal was on her knees, wiping another puddle. "I know, but we can't put him back in the kennel."

"I know. So what do we do?"

"I think he's just anxious. And lonely." She sat back on her heels and looked at Max, who was curled up on the couch.

I followed her gaze. "You think that's it?"

"He's by himself all day. No one to play with. He's gotta be bored."

She was probably right. But knowing didn't solve the problem.

For the next few days, we went in circles. We couldn't leave him alone. We couldn't kennel him. And we couldn't afford to quit our jobs and stay home.

We were exhausted, out of ideas, and something had to change soon.

One evening, I sat at the high bar answering emails while Crystal scrolled through her phone at the kitchen table.

"What if we got him a friend?" she asked, eyes still on her phone.

I turned. "What?"

"Another dog. To keep him company."

I closed my laptop slowly. "You're joking."

"I'm not."

"We can barely handle *one* dog."

"Exactly. One dog is the problem. If he had a friend, maybe he wouldn't destroy everything."

*Is she insane? Probably a little. According to the state of Georgia, she did agree to marry me, after all.*

Two dogs meant double the food, double the vet bills, and double all the other things we weren't thinking about at the moment. And what if they hated each other? What if they fought?

I opened my mouth to argue, but then I stopped. I tried to picture what saying "no" would fix. The answer came fast. Absolutely nothing.

"You're serious about this," I finally said.

She turned toward me. "I don't know what else to do for Max."

*Same.*

Max was lying on the floor between us, chewing on his toy, and had looked up when she said his name.

"If we do this, and it doesn't work—"

"Then we'll figure something else out."

I blew out a long breath. "We're *really* doing this?"

*"Don't put me in my kennel. I wanna sleep with you."*

*"I'm sad when you go to work. So don't do it anymore.
Mmmkay?"*

# 6

# Tug of War

Max's tail stopped mid-wag.

He'd been dancing at the door like always, performing his whole welcome-home routine. But the second his eyes fell to the Morkie in my arms, his ears flattened.

"Hey, boy." I stepped through the front door.

Max stared at the trembling fluff of copper and white hair pressed against me.

I kneeled, and Crystal crouched beside me. I lowered the small dog to the floor. His tiny paws touched down, and his eyes darted between us and Max.

Slowly, Max stepped forward. One paw. Then another. His nose twitched, and he circled once, sniffing the stranger's back, his ears, his tail—and, naturally, his butt. Standard protocol.

The puppy stood perfectly still—more still, at least, than I would've been if anyone were sniffing mine.

When Max completed his inspection, he sat down in front of me and looked up as if to ask, "Who's this, and why's he in my house?"

"Max, this is your brother," Crystal said, placing a hand on the newcomer. "Spartacus."

His former owner had named him Mister Max. (Like Max, he came from a breeder—not a shelter or rescue. I've already said my piece about that, and it still stands. I can't change what I didn't know then, and I'll never regret the dogs who found their way to us.)

Anyway, Mister Max wasn't going to work for obvious reasons. I'd suggested *Spartacus* on the drive over—another famous gladiator. Technically, Spartacus was the real one. Maximus was just Hollywood. But I wasn't about to get into that right now.

Crystal had loved it immediately, but not because she cared about any of that. She'd learned to tune out my history nerd quirks years ago. She just loved a good theme, and this was one she could work with.

My mind drifted to a time earlier that year when I'd been eight hours deep into a *Spartacus* docu-series before I dozed off on the couch. The sound of the front door opening had woken me. I sat up as the British narrator kept droning on about the Third Servile War.

Crystal had appeared in the doorway, arms crossed. Her eyes flicked from the screen to me, and back to the screen again. Then came the inevitable eye roll. "You watch the most boring things."

She'd said it before, probably every time she caught me rewatching this same series.

*Fair point.*

But those "boring things" had helped name our new dog, so really, who's laughing now? She ought to be grateful.

The memory faded as quickly as it had come, replaced by two pairs of eyes studying each other. Neither moved. It looked less like a meet-and-greet and more like the last stand at the O.K. Corral.

Then Max inched forward.

Spartacus backed into the corner.

Max tilted his head.

Spartacus stiffened, a flash of white teeth—then snapped.

Max jumped back and looked at me. He'd never been snapped at before, not by us or anyone else.

"It's okay, boy," I said, though I didn't truly know if it was.

That night, half-distracted by a string of "urgent" work texts that didn't really need me, I heard the sound of soft pattering against the laminate.

I turned.

A puddle was spreading in the corner by the kitchen table.

*Seriously?*

We'd just had him outside ten minutes before. Maybe less.

I grabbed the paper towels and spray cleaner from under the sink and began to clean. I was on the third wad of paper towels when I heard the jingle of Max's collar.

He trotted past me, rubber ring in his mouth, and headed straight for where Spartacus was sitting near the kitchen island. He dropped the ring right in front of him.

Spartacus lunged forward, teeth bared, letting out a sharp bark.

Max launched himself backward, sliding across the floor before catching himself.

For a second, he only stared. Then he picked up his toy, carried it to his bed, and lay down with it between his paws. His eyes stayed locked on Spartacus across the room.

I looked at Spartacus, then at Max, then down at the soggy paper towels in my hand.

*Going great.*

This story repeated itself over the next few days.

I didn't have words for the hurt I felt watching Max—who'd never met a soul he didn't try to befriend—get rejected, again and again, by the dog we'd brought home to keep him company.

Just the week before, we'd been on a walk when he spotted the neighbor's cat sitting in the driveway. Max dropped into a play bow, butt in the air, tail wagging, and let out an excited bark.

The cat had given him a long, unimpressed look before turning and sauntering back toward the porch.

Max stood there, seeming to wait for a different response. It never came. Still, every time he saw that cat, he tried again with the same bow and the same hopeful bark. The outcome hadn't changed.

*Cat's loss, really.*

Then there was Miss Helen, who walked her German Shepherd past our house most mornings right as we were heading out ourselves. The dog was easily three times Max's size, but that didn't stop him. The first time Max spotted him, he lunged so hard he nearly pulled my arm out of its socket.

The Shepherd froze, towering over him, head tilted as if trying to figure out what this tiny creature was. Max barked, then darted around trying to get him to play.

Miss Helen laughed. "Well, he ain't shy, is he?"

That was Max.

As for Spartacus, he was still peeing everywhere and growling at everything, showing zero signs this experiment was working.

I finished cleaning the floor and tossed the paper towels in the trash, wondering what we'd gotten ourselves into.

Days later, I was working from home when I heard a yelp from the kitchen. I ran in and found Max backing away from Spartacus, who was standing over his food bowl, teeth bared. Max looked at me.

"Come here, boy," I said, picking him up.

He buried his face in my neck, and I felt his little heart thump against my chest. I carried him to the couch and sat down with him in my lap. "I'm sorry," I whispered.

I leaned back, letting my head rest against the cushion. I'd read more articles and watched more videos over the past week than I had for my senior thesis in college. But none of it helped in this moment. So I just kept my hand on his back, hoping that would be enough.

When he lifted his head and licked my cheek, I could feel a sort of faith in me I wasn't sure I'd earned. *The Office* was still playing in the background—Michael Scott arguing with Toby—while I wondered how to make things right. Max glanced at the TV, then tucked himself further into my lap, as if nothing had ever been wrong.

That night, Crystal and I lay in bed, both dogs settled in their crates. The house was quiet. I flipped my pillow to the cool side. Adjusted. Flipped it back. I grabbed my phone: *11:50 p.m.*

We'd gone to bed at nine.

Crystal pulled the covers up higher. "Maybe this was a mistake."

I knew what she meant. Probably. I'd gotten in trouble a handful of times for assuming what she was thinking, and also for not knowing what she was thinking. Still, I'd learned it was safer to ask. I turned to face her. "What do you mean?"

"Getting Spartacus." Her voice cracked. "What if he hurts Max?"

I reached for her hand, wanting to tell her she was wrong—that Spartacus just needed time—but I couldn't quite say it. "Yeah."

We both stared at the ceiling.

"So, what do we do?" she asked.

Crystal's question lingered.

Usually, when she asked me things, I had an answer. And if I didn't, I at least knew where to look. Now, whether that answer turned out favorable—that's a different story. Like the time she'd asked me to find a wedding planner. I took a friend's recommendation, and that planner managed to decorate the ballroom in the exact opposite colors Crystal had asked for, lose our cake, forget the silverware—people were eating with their hands—steal a thousand dollars from us, and then for good measure, block us on social media like we'd been the problem.

Though we'd survived that disaster, this one felt different. This time, I didn't have an answer at all.

She squeezed my hand but didn't say anything.

"I don't know," I finally said. "Thought we were doing the right thing for Max."

"But what if we aren't?"

I didn't have an answer for that either.

Light cut across my face. I squinted and turned away from the window.

Blinked.

Listened.

Silence.

I grabbed my phone off the nightstand: *7:00 a.m.*

My body felt lighter than it had in days. No barking, howling, or 3:00 a.m. impromptu trips to the backyard.

*Strange.*

I'd slept through the night. The *entire* night.

I sat up and looked at Crystal. She was still asleep.

*When's the last time this happened?*

I slid out of bed and headed to the kitchen. Both crates sat side by side near the counter. Max's eyes brightened the moment he saw me. Spartacus glanced upward, head resting on his paws.

I crouched and unlatched Max's crate. "Morning, boy."

He stepped out, gave himself a full shake, and padded straight to Spartacus and sat.

I watched him for a beat, then opened Spartacus's crate. He yawned, stepped out, and stretched.

Max's tail whipped back and forth. He grabbed his toy from the floor and brought it over, dropping it between them.

Spartacus sniffed it.

Max nudged it closer, then picked it up again, holding one end in his mouth.

Spartacus glanced at the toy and in an instant, he clamped his teeth around the other side of the ring, and the two of them were tugging in opposite directions.

I straightened.

*Wait. Not fighting?*

When the ring slipped from Spartacus's mouth, Max kept hold of his end, trotting a few steps closer. Spartacus took it again, and soon they were pulling, growling, letting go, starting over.

Then the game changed. Max let the ring fall, then pounced, and the two of them tumbled onto the carpet. Spartacus barked, then flipped onto his back like he was trying out a jiu-jitsu move—paws up, legs kicking. Max circled him a few times before they rolled, twisted, and chased each other until they finally collapsed side by side, panting.

Max looked over at me, tongue hanging out, tail sweeping across the floor.

Something within me eased, and I could only smile, thinking about the miracle I'd witnessed. I exhaled, and my mind wandered to how rarely we love first, or forgive quickly, or keep showing up after disappointment.

Somehow, Max had figured out how to do just that. And maybe, in some small way, so had I.

By the end of the week, you couldn't find one without the other. They napped on the same bed, followed each other from room to room, and discovered they made a pretty effective team when it came to destroying the walls and baseboards.

*Holding Spartacus for the first time.*

*"Hey, who's this new dog???"*

*"I AM SPARTACUS!"*

*"We're kind of best friends now."*

*"Let's rip Mom's sock! She's got plenty."*

*"Teamwork makes the dream work. Mom and Dad can just buy us a new floor after we chew this one up."*

# 7

# Two True Loves

The headset crackled in my ear. "We're outta biscuits. What should we do?"

December 29th began as an ordinary Saturday morning, which at Chick-fil-A meant organized chaos teetering on the brink of complete disaster. The breakfast-to-lunch transition was always the worst. At ten-thirty in the morning, we were slammed from both sides with people desperate for the last chicken biscuit and others already ordering sandwiches and fries.

I stood at the expo station, headset on, watching orders stack up on the screen. Green tickets turned yellow, then red. The drive-thru line wrapped around the building from what I could see on the cameras. Inside, the dining room was packed with overlapping conversations, chairs scraping, kids shouting, and what seemed to be the rise of a hundred voices competing to be heard.

"How many biscuits are we short?" I asked, already doing the math in my head.

*Twenty-two cars in line. Average of two biscuits per order—*

"Kitchen says six minutes on the next batch."

*Six minutes? We'll lose half the line.*

This was the life of an executive director. Fancy title, I know. I should've been in the office, analyzing data and doing the high-leverage work that actually grew the business. Instead, here I was with a grease splatter on my shirt, trying to figure out how to make forty-four biscuits appear out of thin air. If there was ever a moment for all those Tony Robbins "visualize abundance" videos to pay off, this was it.

In my role, I was expected to do both: lead in the trenches *and* in the war room. I considered myself a talented multitasker, but I wasn't a magician. "Tell drive-thru to offer—"

I paused.

*A coupon? A free drink?*

My brain was trying to land on something more solid, but all I could think about were those forty-four imaginary biscuits.

"Wait." Crystal's voice cut through the noise. She was already next to me with that look on her face that meant she had a plan. As the training director, she was technically supposed to be coaching the new team members, but when she saw problems, she fixed them—sometimes before I'd even figured out how to articulate them.

Crystal grabbed the headset at the drive-thru station and moved to the window. "Good morning! We're transitioning to lunch right now, and our last batch of biscuits just sold out. But I've got something even better for you. How about I upgrade you to a chicken sandwich meal for free and throw in a cookie for the wait?"

I watched the camera. The first car hesitated, then the brake lights flicked off and it rolled forward.

She kept going. "Thanks so much for your patience. You're gonna love this sandwich. And by the way, that cookie's still warm."

One by one, the cars went through, and the orders began to clear from the screen. Before I knew it, the line had emptied. Crisis averted. Crystal set down the headset and grinned. She caught my eye as she sauntered to the back. "You're welcome."

I smirked, knowing I was lucky to work alongside her. She certainly had a knack for making the impossible look simple. I exhaled, and for a second, everything felt manageable again. Then—

The screen lit up with new orders, and someone called out from the kitchen. "We need more fries now!"

*Same time every Saturday. Why are we acting surprised?*

At the front counter, a customer leaned over, waving. "Can I get, like, ten more Chick-fil-A sauces? I'm over there."

*For one order of hashbrowns? Just say you want to take some home, lady.*

A hand tugged at my shoulder. I turned to find one of the cashiers. "I got a mobile order here, but the name doesn't match what's on screen. What should I do?"

*What'd you do the last time this happened? An hour ago.*

More people pushed through the front doors. In the drive-thru, cars stacked up one after another. The lunch rush was here. Sometimes it came early, sometimes late, but it always arrived.

My phone buzzed in my pocket three times in quick succession.

*Later.*

The next hour blurred. I expedited orders, restocked the front line, helped a new hire use the ice cream machine, and answered seventeen different questions. The screen cycled through red tickets back to green, then red again. Eleven became noon. Noon became one. Somewhere in there, I'd run to the back and scarfed down old hash-browns over a trash can—my "break" meal. My feet ached. My shirt stuck to my back with sweat. My ear throbbed from the headset pressing on the same spot all morning.

Finally, there was a lull. Not a break—we'd never get an actual break on a Saturday—but a moment where the orders slowed enough that I could step away, pull out my phone, and check the notifications.

*Seven texts. Two missed calls.*

My chest tightened.

Dad never reached out to me during work. Never un-less—

I hurried to the back office before opening the message. The text sat on my phone screen.

> *Lexi's gone. I'm sorry, son.*

I read it once. Then again. I gripped the phone tighter. The screen blurred. Or maybe that was my eyes.

The room tilted and my stomach lurched—actually lurched—the way it does in that first sudden drop on a roller coaster.

I almost threw up.

My body buckled, and I fell onto the plastic chair with no back.

I read it a third time and stared at my phone as if doing so might change the message to be anything other than what it was. The words didn't change, and neither did the photo below them: the eyes of my childhood dog closed as she lay on a blanket, Dad's hand on her side.

The office blurred around me. Everything else disappeared ...

*A puppy on my shoulder, her whole body small enough to perch there, tiny teeth gnawing at my hair while I laughed—*

Gone.

*The way she'd tilt her head during my infomercial impressions, waiting for the punchline—*

Gone.

*The summer of '05, the nightmares, and Lexi licking away tears until I could breathe again—*

Gone.

*Her bursting through my parents' bedroom door, saving me from myself when the cold barrel pressed against my temple—*

Gone.

*Last month, her struggle to stand. White fur where black used to be. Cataracts clouding eyes that once saw everything. Whispering "Lexi, I love you so much" into her ear while already grieving the goodbye—*

Fourteen years together. All of it—

Gone. *Forever.*

... I blinked, and the office rushed back into focus. I folded forward, and my forehead found the desk. Then came the sound, a wail I didn't recognize as my own, like something had been ripped out of me. Tears soaked the papers beneath my face, bleeding the ink into unreadable smears.

I don't know how long I'd cried before the door opened.

"Kerk? What happened?"

I couldn't look at Crystal. Couldn't lift my head. Couldn't do anything but stay slumped over. I heard her footsteps cross the small space and felt her presence beside me. "Lexi," I finally said. "She's gone."

Crystal wrapped her arms around me from behind and held on. When someone tried to enter, she blocked the door.

A few minutes passed before my breathing evened.

"Go home," she said quietly.

I shook my head. What would I even do there? At least here I could stay busy, or pretend to. Right now, pretending sounded better than feeling. "I'm staying."

"Kerk—"

I straightened. "I need to finish."

She studied my face, biting her bottom lip before she spoke. "Okay."

I walked back out front, and before I reached the end of the counter, a customer requested a refill. I got it for them and said, "My pleasure."

The new cashier rang up the wrong order, *again*. I fixed that too.

In the dining room, I smiled at a family and asked if everything was okay with their meal. They said yes. I nodded and moved to the next table.

A team member asked about break rotation. I looked at the schedule and told them who was next. They thanked me. I said something back, but I don't remember what.

Crystal appeared beside me at some point, put her hand on my arm, and asked if I was okay. I said yes. She didn't look convinced.

More orders came in, and more customers filled the restaurant. My hands moved and my mouth formed words. My body performed the tasks it had done a thousand times before.

Before I knew it, the evening shift arrived. I was done. I reviewed the sales projections with the incoming director, then grabbed my bag and headed out the door.

The drive passed in a blur of familiar streets and red lights I don't remember stopping at. The rumble of the engine, the click of the turn signal, the songs on the radio all felt like someone else's life. Still, I ended up in my driveway and sat there for a moment before getting out.

The house looked the same as it had that morning—white siding, black trim, pine straw scattered across the lawn, the bushes lining the front porch, the white vinyl fence that needed pressure washing.

Walking up the driveway, my keys felt heavy in my hand. The concrete path to the porch felt longer than it should have. I unlocked the front door. The deadbolt clicked. The knob turned. When the door swung open, I stepped inside and made it exactly three feet before my legs gave out. I collapsed to the floor, right there in the entryway.

And that's when they came.

Max hit me first with his frantic energy, climbing into my lap. Spartacus was right behind him, gentler but just as insistent, tucking himself against my side. I wrapped my arms around both of them and sobbed.

They didn't get distracted by the strange sounds I was making, or a toy, or anything else. They just stayed close, absorbing every tear and every piece of grief I couldn't hold inside anymore.

Eventually, rational thought returned and reminded me I'd known this was coming. My parents had warned me that Lexi was declining fast. They'd even asked if I wanted to come say goodbye one last time. I'd said no—not because I didn't love her, but because I wasn't strong enough to watch her die. I told myself it was easier this way.

It wasn't easier.

I should've been there. That's the one regret I'll carry forever.

Spartacus stretched and trotted to his water bowl. Max pulled back just enough to look at me. Our eyes locked, and in that moment, I made a promise to him and to myself.

I would *never* make that mistake again.

When it was his turn—and I hated even thinking about it—I would be there. I would hold him and make sure he knew he was loved right up to his last breath. Max's eyes stayed fixed on mine, as if my presence at the very end was already a certainty he'd never questioned.

My legs began to go numb beneath me. I shifted, and Max hopped down. Using the entryway table, I pulled myself up from the hard floor. The couch was only a few steps away. I made it there and sank into the cushions.

Both dogs jumped up beside me. I pulled out my phone and opened the photos app, though every logical part of me knew this was a terrible idea. But I needed to see her face.

The tears came again as I scrolled through the pictures. Max climbed onto my chest and stayed there.

I stopped scrolling.

I closed my eyes and let myself feel this entire moment—his heart beat against mine, the rise and fall of his breath, the warmth of his small body. I rested my hand on his side, feeling his ribs expand and contract. We stayed like that until my eyes grew too heavy to hold open and the phone slipped from my hand.

Sundays were intended to be off days at Chick-fil-A. The whole company closed so everyone could rest, spend time with family, and go to church if that was their thing.

But if you were on the leadership team, "off" just meant you worked from home.

I sat at my kitchen table with my laptop open, staring at a spreadsheet for Monday's meeting. Numbers blurred together, and though I'd read the same column three times, I still couldn't tell you what it said.

Crystal stood at the stove, flipping pancakes. The smell of batter hitting the hot griddle filled the kitchen. I wasn't hungry, though I hadn't eaten since those hashbrowns over the trash can yesterday.

She set a plate and a fork in front of me; three golden brown pancakes, stacked with butter melting between the layers, and not a single burned spot.

Before Chick-fil-A, I'd been at Waffle House for seven years, working my way up to a district manager position. While there, I'd learned the "secret" was to use half and half instead of water in the mix. I'd shared that with Crystal, and then she'd perfected it beyond anything I'd ever seen over the years. Every single time, hers came out just right.

"Eat," she said.

I nodded but didn't pick up my fork.

My phone was face-down next to my laptop. It had buzzed twice since I sat, and I'd pushed it farther away each time. Now it was at the end of the table. My hand hovered over it once, out of muscle memory, to check; but I pulled back. If I flipped it over, I'd see messages. If I saw messages, I might start browsing my apps. Maybe the photo app. And if I opened my photos ...

I left it face-down.

In the living room, another rerun of *The Office* played; I wasn't watching it, but Michael Scott's voice carried into the kitchen. Season one, episode two. Or maybe three. The occasional jingle of dog tags added to the ambiance as Max and Spartacus moved around somewhere behind me. These were the sounds of a normal Sunday.

Even so, today felt like something else, like the world had dimmed a notch and I was moving through it from an arm's length away. I forced myself to click through the same tabs—staffing projections, sales data, operations notes—catching pieces of information here and there, staring at charts I could normally read in seconds. My eyes skimmed the numbers again, but nothing stuck. It was important work, the kind that kept the business running, but one thought drowned out the rest:

*Who cares? Lexi just died.*

I'd thought about asking for time off, just a few days to gather myself. But the last time I'd requested time off months ago, it had been approved with a long pause followed by a slight tightening around the operator's mouth. "Well, I mean, of course you *can*." Then came the barrage of questions about coverage and about whether I'd thought through the impact on the team.

Then there was the time Max got sick. Really sick. Like vomiting, lethargic, and not eating kind of sick. Crystal couldn't take him to the vet because she'd gotten called into work, so I'd asked to leave early.

"Of course you *can*," he'd said over the phone. "I mean, he's your dog." A pause. "It's just ... we've got a big catering order coming up. They might need your help." Another pause. "But if your dog *really* needs you ..."

Before I left, I'd made sure the team had everything they needed for the large order. I called the operator back to let him know everything was set and that I'd call the store later to check on the order.

He sighed. "Don't worry about it. I'll just check on it myself."

*Yeah. Glad you're worried about Max.*

I'd seen what had happened to others who'd needed time off, or said no to extra shifts, or mentioned burnout. Their names stopped coming up in promotion conversations, and suddenly they weren't "culture fits."

So naturally, I said yes to everything.

I'd thought about quitting several times before, but I couldn't afford to. There were times though, I had imagined how this place would function if something terrible happened to me. After running through every scenario, ultimately, I'd come to this conclusion: If I didn't show up tomorrow, they'd shuffle the schedule, customers would keep coming, and despite the years I put into this place, within a month, most people wouldn't even remember I'd been there.

It was a tough truth, and still, I was sitting here reviewing a spreadsheet about chicken sandwich sales instead of grieving the loss of my childhood dog.

*How'd I end up here?*

I reached for the trackpad, and my finger traced circles on it, moving the cursor back and forth across the screen, going nowhere.

Something soft nudged my leg. I looked down.

*Max.*

His ring toy was clamped in his mouth, and his tail wagged slowly before he dropped it at my feet. He stared up at me with those dark eyes, as if he knew I needed this even more than he did.

I closed the laptop, then slid off the chair and sat on the floor. Max immediately climbed onto me. His little body nestled against my chest. I draped an arm around him. For a moment, I just breathed.

Max squirmed free, grabbed the ring, and shoved it into my hand. I tugged gently, and he pulled back, growling playfully. And sitting there on the laminate, watching Max refuse to let go of his toy, something inside me shifted.

I'd never thought I'd have another dog like Lexi. Never thought I could. She'd been everything to me through the good times and the ones when I thought I didn't have a reason to keep living.

But here was Max, a different dog with a different kind of love.

And that didn't diminish what Lexi had meant to me. It didn't replace her or erase her. Both things were true at the same time: I could grieve what was lost and still make room in my heart for what was right in front of me.

Max dropped the ring and tilted his head. Our eyes met. I smiled.

And for the first time since yesterday, I felt something other than grief.

I felt grateful.

*Lexi and seventeen-year-old me.*

*My sweet Lexi and her pink bandana.*

*"Did you say, SNACKS???"*

*Photobooth at a Chick-fil-A work event.*

# 8

# The Stray

**Year Two**

## 2019

A PUPPY LAY ALONE near the entrance of a car dealership. Maybe eight weeks old, ribs showing through a patchy black coat. Summer heat radiated off the asphalt, but he didn't move. Still, people stepped over this living being on their way inside.

*Stepped over.*

*What if this were Max?*

I stopped. The puppy's eyes were barely open, and when they found mine, I kneeled. Up close, a small wound marked his face, and dozens of fleas hopped along his fur.

*How long has he been here? Hours? Days?*

When I reached out to touch him, his eyes lit up, just barely, but enough to let me know he'd been waiting to be seen by someone, anyone. I brushed my hand down his back, and fleas jumped onto my arm. Slapping them away, I refocused on this tiny creature, who'd somehow ended up abandoned in this parking lot.

*Looks hungry.*

When I turned, he'd followed me. At the car, he lay at my feet and gazed up at me. I fed him my chicken strips that I had never gotten a chance to eat that day. He scarfed it down as a voice called out. "Kerk?" The salesperson had finally appeared. "You ready?"

I'd come to sign paperwork for Crystal's new black and red Jeep she'd been wanting for months. I looked at my new friend, then at the salesperson. "I'll have to come back another day."

Her face fell, but I was already crouching again. "All right, friend. You ready to go?"

I opened the passenger door, and he jumped right in, settling onto the seat. From the driver's side, I got in and cranked the AC, angling the vents toward him. Cool air hit his face, and he leaned into it, mouth open, ears blown back, trying to catch the wind.

Then he turned and looked at me in the kind of way that made me believe this moment was always meant to happen.

At home, I filled a spare dog bowl with water and set it down in the garage. He approached cautiously, sniffed once, then gulped it down. From inside the house, Max and Spartacus erupted in barking. "Hold on, boys!"

I grabbed the old hose and turned it on. The puppy tried to run when the water hit him, but I gently steadied him, working methodically to wash away every flea. "It's okay," I kept saying. "You're gonna feel better soon."

When we finally finished, I wrapped him in a beach towel and held him close. His eyes met mine, and he smiled.

Actually smiled.

I pulled out my phone and took a photo of him, staring at me like I'd saved his life. Which, I suppose, I had. A lump rose in my throat, and my eyes filled before I could stop it. The blur thickened until I had to blink to see him clearly.

*Why do terrible things happen to innocent animals?*

I stopped the thought before it could fully form. Sometimes there aren't any good answers to questions like that. I've learned not to look for them.

So instead, I focused on the dog in my arms and held him until he fell asleep. A sadness fell over me knowing that Crystal and I couldn't keep him. We were already stretched thin with Max and Spartacus. I knew I had to find him another home.

Within an hour of posting on Facebook, a woman named Sandy responded. She had another dog who needed a companion. She seemed promising, so I agreed to meet up and didn't charge her anything. I was just happy he'd found a home.

When she arrived, she had a warm smile and a gentle way about her. She didn't rush, letting him sniff her hand first, and spoke to him in a soft voice. Though you never really know who people are behind closed doors, something in my gut told me he'd be okay with her. So I handed him over, kissed his head one last time, and watched her drive away into the dusk. I'd never rescued an animal before, and it gave me a feeling I still can't fully describe.

Looking back now, I realize how lucky I got with Sandy. She was exactly who she seemed to be. But I've since learned that there are people who search for free animals online and use them as bait in dog fighting rings, or worse. It's one of the reasons rescue organizations always charge adoption fees, to protect the animals from evildoers who see "free" as an opportunity.

I know better now.

A week later, I was walking to my car after work when my phone buzzed.

*A Facebook message from Sandy.*

I slid into the seat, closed the door, and opened the message.

*Hey, Kerk. I'm so sorry to have to tell you this, but Gunner passed away.*

My chest tightened.

*We did everything we could to save him, taking him to the vet countless times. He was having seizures and wasn't eating. We found out he had parvo, two types of worms, and an intestinal infection. We did everything we could.*

The words didn't make sense at first. I read them again. Then again.

A ringing started in my ears.

My fingers went numb.

The phone grew heavy in my hand.

My grip loosened, and it fell.

The parking lot outside the windshield seemed far away.

All I could see were his eyes looking up at me from that beach towel, and the way he'd fallen asleep in my arms. Everything inside me spilled out.

I sat there long enough for my eyes to dry and for the sun to set.

When I finally made it home, I walked through the door and sank onto the couch. Max was there and climbed onto me, nudging himself against my chest. Spartacus settled in close, resting his head on my thigh. In the stillness, the thoughts crept in.

*Should've taken him to a vet immediately.*

*Should've done more.*

Over the following months, I couldn't stop thinking about Gunner. I wanted to help other animals like him, and donating to a local animal rescue seemed like the first step.

*Simple enough.*

After work one night, I sat on the couch with a PB&J and my laptop open. I pulled up the rescue's website, clicked *Donate*, and reached for my wallet. Before entering my card number, I checked our account balance.

*$23.00.*

I checked savings.

*$0.00*

I sat back and stared at the screen. I had just enough to cover the water bill.

*Where'd it all go?*

The answer was parked in the garage: a Hellcat, a custom Viper, and a new Jeep.

I looked down at the tattoos covering my arms and chest.

*Ten grand—at least.*

I glanced down the hall at the rooms we rarely stepped foot in.

*What was I thinking?*

Those things seemed important once.

*Dual-income couple with no kids—and nothing to give.*

I sighed.

A jingling sound pulled me back.

I looked up. Max and Spartacus were standing there, tails wagging, ready to go outside. I moved my laptop and set my plate on the coffee table. I made it two steps before I stopped.

*Better take it with me.*

I grabbed the plate, and when I opened the door, a chilly breeze brushed past. Max paused, eyeing my dinner.

"Not this time."

He gave it one last glance and then followed Spartacus outside.

I smiled and leaned against the doorframe before taking a bite. Sweet strawberry jelly hit my tongue, and crunchy peanut butter clung to the roof of my mouth. In the yard, crickets chirped, and the boys chased each other from one corner of the fence to the other. I took a slow breath and set the sandwich back on the plate.

Above me, the sky had turned that deep shade of blue right before the night takes over. A few stars were beginning to show. I searched for the Big Dipper.

*Found it. Or is that the Little Dipper?*

I scanned further until landing on a bright one lower on the horizon.

*Venus, maybe. Or it could be—*

Something slammed against my leg, knocking me a half step sideways. I looked down just in time to see Max mid-landing, eyes locked on my plate. I held it higher, completely out of reach. "That's a no-no."

He sat at my feet, glaring as if I were the unreasonable one.

*Never gonna change.*

I shook my head, and my thoughts floated somewhere else ...

About a week after Lexi passed, I was on the couch one evening with a bowl of chili, watching the Ken Burns Civil War documentary. I'd seen it a dozen times, and I think I enjoyed the soundtrack more than the actual content. Something about string music from that era really does it for me. I could hear the narrator talking, but the words weren't sticking as *Ashokan Farewell* swelled through the speakers.

*A violin, definitely. Maybe a viola too. And there's the cello.*

I tried to pick them apart and follow each one separately. Then—

*Ring-Ring-Ring*

"Hold on, Max."

*Ring-Ring-Ring.*

I sat up and turned. Not Max.

*Spartacus.*

He raised his paw and hit the doggy doorbells again. I did a double-take.

*Did that just happen?*

For weeks, Spartacus had been having accidents daily. Multiple times a day. We'd tried everything from puppy pads, training bells, to taking him out every hour. Nothing had worked. It got so bad that we'd even subscribed to Amazon for bulk paper towels for the cleanup. And I hate subscriptions. But we'd had no choice.

Max rounded the kitchen island and trotted over to join his brother at the door. I set my chili bowl on the coffee table and hurried over. I kneeled and scratched behind

Spartacus's ear. "Good boy." His tail wagged, and the second I opened the door, he darted into the backyard.

I stood in the doorway, squinting into the darkness beyond the porch light. For a moment, nothing. Then I caught a flash of white moving near the back fence.

*There he is. Where's Max?*

*Jingle-Jingle-Jingle.*

The sound of dog tags. Too close.

Then a crash.

I spun around.

Max had knocked the chili off the table. His entire face was buried in what was left of it.

"Max!"

He looked up, startled, chili dripping from his snout.

Our eyes met.

I quick-stepped toward him, and he did what he'd always done when caught in the act.

He launched himself off the floor, landed on the couch, bounced to the side table, knocked over the lamp, hit the floor, and bolted for the back door. He streaked past me into the yard before I could fully process what had happened.

My eyes swept the room.

*Chili on the rug.*

*Chili on the cushions.*

*Chili on the laptop.*

I traced the trail across the floor and through the doorway. I muttered a curse.

*I'll clean up in a minute.*

I walked out into the yard, pulling the door closed behind me. As the winter air stung my face, I saw Max in the far corner, already peeing, and probably hoping I'd forget about his most recent sin. Spartacus was still doing laps around the same patch of grass he always fixated on, refusing to go. This was the pattern every single time. He'd go outside, sniff around for ten minutes, then run back in and pee on the floor.

*Can't keep doing this.*

I crossed my arms and watched him shuffle around a beat longer.

*Should've grabbed a jacket.*

And for whatever reason, it hit me then.

*Maybe he's a visual learner.*

Max ambled back to me, chili still coating his snout, and sat at my feet.

"You're in trouble," I said, though I wasn't really sure what that meant. Neither did he, apparently. I let the thought go.

When I moved across the yard toward Spartacus, cold grass crunched under my feet. He glanced up at me—as if *I* were interrupting *him*—then went right back to his search for Atlantis.

"Spartacus, sit, boy." I scanned left, then right. "I need you to watch."

Without delay, he moved closer and then sat. I peeked back at the house and then at the fence. No one could see.

*Alright.*

My hand moved downward, and I hooked my thumb under the elastic band of my sweatpants.

*Wait. Could I end up on some kind of registry for this?*

My pulse quickened. I glanced around again.

*No. This is my yard. My property. There's a six-foot vinyl fence. And it's dark. It's fine. Totally fine.*

So, with logical reassurance, I took one last breath. Then I did it.

A stream hit the grass, louder than I expected. Steam rose, and a puddle formed in front of me.

Spartacus observed, head tilted, as if I were delivering some sort of TED Talk.

*Maybe it's working.*

The back door yanked open, and I flinched, barely managing to aim away from my own feet. Crystal appeared on the porch, catching me midstream. "Kerk ... what are you doing?"

I could only imagine what was going through her mind: her husband, pants down, peeing in the yard, chili smeared across Max's face, and the disaster in the living room behind her.

I felt like Greg in that scene from *Meet the Fockers* where the family comes home and he's wearing moose ears and Jack's artificial feeding breast, while the baby's hands are glued to a bottle of tequila.

No explanation could make this look normal.

Still, I mustered up enough focus and finished, which, given the circumstances, was kind of impressive. I exhaled, and a second later, Spartacus sniffed around where I had just gone.

He circled once—then squatted and began to pee.

*...Jingle-Jingle-Jingle.*

I blinked, and the memory faded, but the feeling stayed with me. The boys scurried through the door and into the house. I was still standing on the porch, sandwich plate in hand, staring at the spot where Max had just been.

The cold settled into my arms, and my breath drifted out in little clouds that disappeared as quickly as they formed. I looked up at the stars one more time. My mind wandered back to Gunner and to the question I still didn't have an answer for: *How am I supposed to help animals when I have nothing to give?*

Maybe I didn't need to have the answer right now.

Still, a piece of me envied Max's carefree approach to living. To him, food was life, and he never seemed to worry about how he'd steal ours. And if he had been, he surely didn't confide in us. No matter what new safeguards we put in place, he always found a way to get it done—even if it meant using his brother as a decoy. And if Spartacus was part of tonight's chili heist from the start, we technically had a conspiracy on our hands.

I smiled at the thought of Max facilitating organized crime, then turned and shut the door behind me. At the counter, he was already pacing, eyes up, scanning for anything he might enjoy. I bit back a laugh.

*Of course.*

Max moved with the kind of certainty that only comes from believing things *will* work out.

If I had the faith of that little black dog, maybe I'd find a way too.

*My new friend.*

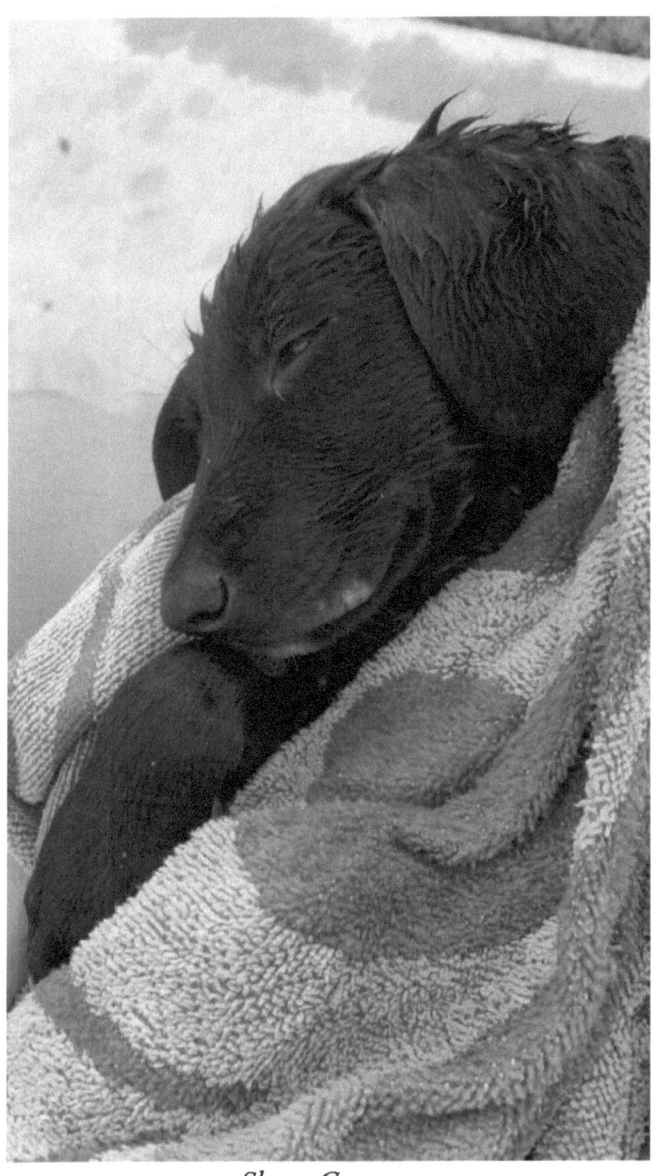

*Sleepy Gunner.*

*"We should be using the bathroom, but this is more fun."*

# 9

# Lexi's Legacy

## Year Three

## 2020

SUSAN'S VOICE CAME THROUGH the laptop speakers. "We couldn't have done this without you."

Behind her, I could see the rescue's back office: mismatched filing cabinets, a corkboard pinned with adoption photos, bags of kibble stacked against the wall, and a heater oscillating in the corner.

"Twenty thousand dollars," the rescue's founder continued, "and all those supplies. Our foster families are going to cry when they see this."

On my screen, six other faces smiled back from their tiny Zoom squares: volunteers, board members, and some others from Susan's team. None I'd met in person, but it felt like I'd known them much longer than I had.

In my lap, Max positioned himself so his head was now visible on camera.

Smiles broke out across the screen. "There he is!" someone said. Several hands waved.

Max studied the screen with the intensity of someone being asked to identify a suspect in a lineup. I'd never actually witnessed one, but thanks to Crystal's weekly crime drama rotation, I felt reasonably qualified to know what one might look like. I lifted his paw and waved it back. He let me, though his expression suggested he was merely tolerating the gesture. "It was a team effort," I said. "I just helped connect the dots."

"Yeah, Team Kerk." Susan chuckled. "That was our biggest fundraiser since opening."

Warmth bloomed on my cheeks. I scratched behind Max's ears, and he leaned into my hand.

Another voice chimed in—Marcy, who ran their social media and also sat on the board. "Before we leave, can I recap the agenda for next week's meeting so we're all on the same page?"

"Sure," I said, pulling up my notes on a separate tab.

"We've got a few priorities. First, we need to get more people sharing our content, not just liking it. Second, we're trying to boost volunteer sign-ups for the spring events. Third, we need to reach out for local business partnerships. And last—" She paused. "Overall, we've been hitting the donation angle pretty hard, but we need to broaden our messaging."

"That's right," I said. "We gotta show people there's other ways to support: volunteering, fostering, sharing posts, and donating supplies. Some folks can't give money right now, and that's okay. We need to make sure they still feel like they're part of this."

A few heads nodded.

"I'll send over a revised messaging doc by Friday," I added. "We can tweak it from there."

We said our goodbyes with the usual pleasantries and, one by one, the squares disappeared until it was only me. Max stretched and hopped off my lap.

I closed the laptop and turned in my chair, letting my gaze drift across the living room. There, on the wall, hung a canvas picture of eight-grade me with Chelsea, our family dog. Next to that, Lexi's memorial box with her collar and some photos. One the other end, a photo of me holding Gunner and painting of Maximus and Spartacus. And in the very center it all, Lexi's pink bandana above a mounted piece of wood that read: *The Lexi's Legacy Foundation.*

I took it in for a moment.

But I didn't let myself look too long. Only long enough to feel proud of what their memories had become—not long enough to fall apart.

Some days, it still didn't feel real.

I pulled up my calendar on the laptop. Colored blocks filled every square with Zoom calls, planning meetings, and a donor event I still needed to prep for. I clicked over to the spreadsheet. Rows and rows of rescue names stretched downward, each one paired with the dollars given and supplies delivered.

*Nearly fifty rescues.*

I scrolled to the bottom.

*$94,847.*

Thoughts of Lexi and Gunner came the same way they always did when I looked at those numbers.

*They'd be proud.*

We'd survived the first six months. More than survived, really. We were actually making a difference.

When I'd started The Lexi's Legacy Foundation, I had no idea what I was doing. Getting our 501(c)(3) status made me feel like this was official, which it was. Even so, I had zero connections in the rescue community, and everything had to be built from scratch. I wasn't completely alone though. Crystal, as always, supported by becoming the Vice President, bringing everything together from behind the scenes. Even Max, who couldn't legally join the board of directors, contributed in his own way. His practical advice was limited as he mostly preferred begging for snacks rather than participating in our meetings. Still, he seemed to know this whole thing would work out long before I did.

My phone buzzed, and I glanced at the screen.

*On my one off day?*

I let it ring.

*I'll call back. Eventually.*

I knew I would. I had to, since it was my boss. But right now, I just needed another minute in a world where I wasn't an executive director managing someone else's dreams.

The truth was, without Chick-fil-A, there'd probably be no Lexi's Legacy Foundation. The skills I'd developed there—leading teams, financial management, and operational efficiency—had turned out to be exactly what struggling rescues needed.

One of the biggest problems I encountered, over and over, was founders who were passionate about animals but had never learned how to run the business side of their organizations. They'd rescue a hundred cats and dogs and have no idea how to track expenses or even manage month-to-month cash flow. Some would host adoption events with no follow-up systems to land potential fosters or adopters. And several would burn out because they didn't know how to delegate or recruit volunteers.

That's where Lexi's Legacy came in. We were a support arm like Lexi had been for me, all those years ago. We donated money and supplies, yes, but also helped these organizations operationalize their missions from strategic planning, system implementation, and fundraising.

The phone buzzed again—a voicemail notification this time.

I sighed.

I wished I had more time in the day to dedicate to this work instead of spreadsheets about chicken sandwich projections. But the reality was, I couldn't afford to walk away from my full-time job. Not yet. Maybe never.

I picked up my phone to check the voicemail. But before I could tap play, the screen lit up with its background image.

*Gunner.*

I stared at the photo—an old friend wrapped in that beach towel, looking up at me with those eyes the day I'd found him.

*Woof! Woof!*

I looked up.

Max stood at the edge of the living room, tail wagging. Beside him, Spartacus sat, looking out the window.

Max barked again.

"Alright, alright." I set my phone on the desk and pushed back from the chair. "Wanna go on a walk?"

Max's whole body launched into one of those full-on shakes that started at his head and didn't stop until it reached the tip of his tail. For a second, he was nothing but a black blur and jingling tags. Spartacus rose to his feet and eased into a slow downward dog position, then lifted into a gentle arch.

I grinned and grabbed their leashes from the hook by the door. Whatever my boss needed could wait another thirty minutes.

The next morning, I stood at the expo station with my headset on, watching orders cycle through the screen. The breakfast rush had peaked, and we were coasting into the transition period.

*Perfect morning.*

"Kerk." A hand tapped my arm.

I turned to find Josie, one of the shift leads. "Yeah?"

"He wants to see you in the office."

I didn't have to ask who "he" was.

I handed Josie my headset and made my way through the kitchen, past the fryers and the prep station, and past the walk-in cooler that always smelled like damp cardboard. The office door was cracked open. I knocked twice and pushed it the rest of the way.

The operator kept his eyes on the computer. "Close it."

I did and then took the seat across from him.

He clicked the mouse a few times. "How's everything going?"

*Everything ... What do you really want?*

"Drive-thru times are down, and we're ahead on food costs for the month, and the new hires are—"

"Good. And that nonprofit of yours?" He started scrolling. "Still keeping you busy?"

I paused. He'd never asked about it before. "It's going well. Just finished up a campaign that raised twenty grand for a rescue in Oregon. And we're about to cross a hundred thousand in total donations and services since we started."

His eyebrows lifted slightly before settling back into place. "Hmmm."

*Okay?*

"Well, that's nice," he said, still focused on the screen. "As long as it doesn't interfere with things here."

*There it is.*

"It won't."

"Good." He reached for a pen and tapped it against the desk in that familiar two-bit rhythm. "Anything else going on I should know about?"

*Am I in trouble?*

My heart jumped fast enough that I felt it in my throat. I scanned the past week in a flash.

*Did I miss something? A shift issue? A guest complaint? Something with corporate?*

My stomach tightened, even as I mentally ran through everything again. Nothing stood out—at least nothing I knew of. The tension slowly loosened in my shoulders, and I let out a breath.

*Here goes nothing.*

My mouth opened, then closed again.

This probably wasn't the moment. Then again, when would be? I'd been sitting on this idea for weeks, wondering if it was crazy or not. Crystal thought I should go for it. Max, of course, had no opinion on the matter, though he'd yawned and walked away when I mentioned it, which I chose to interpret as confidence in my abilities.

"Well," I said, "there is one thing."

He looked up finally.

"I've been thinking about writing a book."

Silence.

"A book," he repeated. Not a question.

"About the dogs in my life. I think it could raise awareness and more money for the animals."

He just stared for a beat, then tilted his head like he was doing mental math and the numbers weren't quite adding up. "*You're* writing a book?"

*Tell me what you really think.*

"Yeah. I am."

He leaned back in his chair. "Have you written anything before?"

"Not professionally. Just my thesis back in—"

"Got a publisher?"

"Not yet."

"Agent?"

"No."

His eyes flicked to his laptop before coming back to me. "And you're going to do this while running a restaurant?"

"That's the plan."

He gave two slow nods. "Sounds like quite the undertaking."

"I'll manage."

"Hmm." He was already typing again.

*Good talk.*

I stood, moved the chair back under the desk, and headed for the door.

"Kerk."

I turned.

"Regional call at two. I'll need those labor projections before then."

"You'll have them."

*The Wall*

*Delivering supplies to a local shelter.*

*I'm so grateful for my friend Micah, who was our very first volunteer. She has done so much for us from delivering supplies to fundraising. Over the years, she's helped raise thousands for Lexi's Legacy through her YouTube channel. Thank you believing in us, Micah! Feel free to check out her YouTube: @JunkyardMook*

*Our volunteers at the Lexi's Legacy blanket drive for the Savannah Humane Society.*

# 10

# Just This Once

THE CURSOR BLINKED AT me.

I sat on the futon in our spare room, laptop balanced on my thighs, staring at the top line, which read: *Untitled Dog Book.* Beneath it were a few small paragraphs I'd written an hour earlier.

I deleted a sentence, then rewrote it: *Lexi changed my life.*

I read it back.

*Boring.*

I tried again: *Lexi changed my life in ways I'm still trying to understand.*

*Ugh. Sounds like a therapy journal.*

I highlighted the line and typed over it: *Lexi made me believe I could be loved without earning it.*

I read it aloud this time.

*Way too much for page one.*

A curse slipped, and I hit delete again.

On the floor, Spartacus lay curled in a half-ball. His copper and white body rose and fell with each slow breath. He'd been asleep for the past two hours. Every now and then, his legs would twitch, probably chasing something in his dreams.

*More productive than what I'm doing.*

The total word count caught my eye: *312*

I checked the clock at the bottom right of the screen.

*Really?*

I'd been at it for four hours.

*Four hours.*

That was roughly seventy-eight words per hour. At this pace, the book would take me approximately six hundred and forty hours to write.

*Great. Should be done by 2037.*

I rubbed my eyes and leaned back against the cushion. The ceiling had a water stain in the corner I'd never noticed before.

*Need to get that looked at.*

Its shape vaguely resembled a Brontosaurus. Or maybe a cloud. Or maybe I was losing my mind.

Outside, the afternoon sky had faded from bright yellow to amber to something dimmer.

I stared at the blank space on the screen.

*What am I doing!?*

I wasn't a writer. I'd never been a writer. The last time I'd written anything longer than an email was the college thesis I'd barely passed. I ran a Chick-fil-A. I knew how to manage labor costs, food inventory, and drive-thru times. I organized fundraising campaigns for animal rescues.

None of that qualified me to write a book.

My operator's voice drifted back to me. *You're writing a book?*

I closed my eyes.

Maybe he'd been right and this whole thing was ridiculous.

The futon creaked, and I opened my eyes again.

Max had jumped up—I hadn't even heard him come into the room—but instead of curling up beside me like he usually did, he climbed onto my back and settled there.

"What are you doing, boy?"

He didn't answer, obviously. He just craned his head forward at the screen.

I forced a smile. "You proofreading now?"

His chin rested on my shoulder. I could feel his breath against my ear.

I looked at the screen again. At the cursor. At the three hundred and twelve words that weren't good enough. At the title that didn't exist and the story I didn't know how to tell. My eyes began to fill, and my vision blurred.

*I can't do this.*

The words were there somewhere, rattling around in my skull. But they weren't coming out right.

Max shifted on my back, and I felt his weight redistribute. His face appeared beside mine. Those big, dark eyes were inches from my own, studying me the way he always did when something was wrong. Or when I had a sandwich. Hard to tell sometimes.

I wiped my cheek with the back of my hand. "I'm okay, boy."

He didn't look away.

There was something in his gaze that I'd seen a hundred times before but couldn't quite name. It wasn't pity. It wasn't even sympathy, not really. It was simpler than that. It felt as if he were saying, "You can do this, Daddy."

I didn't believe what Max seemed so certain of, though I wanted to. But he was still there. Watching.

So, I took a breath and focused on the screen. I placed my fingers on the keyboard and started typing.

A cohesive sentence formed.

*Not bad.*

Then another.

*I like it.*

And before I knew it, a new paragraph had taken shape.

The word count climbed: *350. 400. 450.*

Outside, the last of the light had faded, and the room went dark except for the glow of the laptop screen. Max's breathing slowed against my neck. He'd fallen asleep in the narrow space between my back and the futon cushion. I don't know how to explain it, but somehow, from then on, the words just flowed more easily.

So, I kept writing.

Later that night, Crystal and I stood in the kitchen, guiding the boys into their kennels. Spartacus went first, stepping inside without fuss and turning before nestling into his blanket. Crystal gave him a scratch before latching the door.

Max required more convincing. He stood at the kennel entrance, staring at it like I'd just asked him to walk into prison willingly for the next fifteen years.

"Come on, boy." I crouched beside him. "Night-night time."

He looked at me. Then at the kennel. Then back at me. *Not this again.*

I was too tired to negotiate, so I did what every dog parent knows to do: I reached for a treat and tossed it inside.

Was I being an enabler? Absolutely.

Did I care? Not at 11:00 p.m. on a work night.

Max darted in, snatched it, and immediately tried to bolt back out. I was quicker. The latch clicked shut.

"Night-night, boy."

He gave me a look that suggested I'd hear about this later.

In bed, I kept my eyes closed, listening to Crystal's slow breathing beside me.

*I love that for her.*

I pulled the blanket up. Pushed it down. Kicked one leg out. Rolled onto my side. Then my back. Then my side again. Onto my stomach. Sat up. Adjusted the pillow. Flipped it over.

Nothing was working.

The writing session had ended up being somewhat productive. More words than I'd expected. But now, lying here, all I could think about was everything I still had to do.

*Don't know how to finish the book.*

*Pages of unanswered Lexi's Legacy emails.*

*Work tomorrow.*

*Same for the day after that and—*

My chest tightened.

*How am I supposed to do all of this?*

I tried to count the ceiling fan blades as they spun to slow my thoughts, but lost track before the third rotation.

The question spiraled, picking up speed.

My heart pounded against my ribs. A strange lightness crept into my head. The walls swayed around me, even though I hadn't moved.

I don't know if I said it out loud or just channeled my thoughts in the direction of up. But somewhere in the dark, I asked for help and then started counting breaths.

"One. Two. Three. Four. One. Two. Three. Four."

It seemed to help, but only a little. And then—

*Jingle-Jingle-Jingle.*

The spiral stopped.

Crystal snapped upright. "Did you hear that?"

My thoughts steadied just enough. "Yeah."

We both glanced at the closed bedroom door, then back to each other.

*Jingle-Jingle-Jingle.*

Frantic scratching against the wood followed.

"What the—" I threw off the covers and crossed the room. When I opened the door, Max shot through like he'd been fired from a cannon. He launched himself onto the bed, rolled around, and plopped down between our pillows.

Crystal and I looked at each other, thinking the same thing.

*How did he ...*

I walked down the hall to the kitchen and flipped on the light. Max's kennel sat exactly where we'd left it. The door was wide open.

Spartacus looked up at me from inside his kennel, blinking in the sudden brightness, as if to say, "I had nothing to do with this."

I crouched and examined the scene.

*Latch looks intact. Did I not close it all the way?*

Footsteps approached from behind. "Well?"

"I could've sworn I latched it. I remembered the click. But maybe I'd imagined it. Or maybe—"

"No, no ..." Crystal shook her head. "I mean, is that even possible?"

"Theoretically, everything's possible. Gravity's technically a theory and also—"

She groaned. "Okay, nerd. I get it."

The jingle-jangle of Max's tags drifted from the bedroom, pulling our attention toward the doorway.

Crystal turned to me with that familiar look. "Maybe they could sleep with us tonight. Just this once."

I considered the unintended consequences, but not for long. A part of me knew how this would end.

"Just this once," I repeated.

The next morning, I woke to sunlight on my face. Birds chirped outside the window, and the faint jingling of tags carried from down the hall. I stretched, pushed myself up, swung my legs off the bed, and made my way to the kitchen.

By the backdoor, Max threw a paw over his brother before Spartacus wriggled free and pounced back. They darted to the kitchen island, pausing at the corners to peek and outmaneuver each other—Max going left when Spartacus expected right, then Spartacus doubling back with surprising speed.

I took a second to appreciate the spectacle. Two brothers, happy and exactly where they belonged.

When I opened the door, they exploded into the yard. Max tore across the grass in a wide arc while Spartacus followed at his own pace. I stepped out onto the porch for a moment, watching them play, then turned toward the kitchen to start breakfast. I opened the fridge and weighed my options.

Eggs?

*Too much effort.*

Yogurt?

*Maybe if I were a better person.*

Bread?

*French toast, maybe? No—just eggs with extra steps.*

*But regular toast ...*

I reached for the bread and dropped two slices into the toaster. The click of the lever stirred childhood nostalgia.

*Brave Little Toaster. Totally underrated movie. Haven't seen that since—*

"Kerk!"

My heart shot into overdrive as I sprinted down the hall, mentally preparing for blood, broken glass, an intruder, or even one of those monstrous Middle Eastern spiders. By the time I reached the doorway, I was breathing hard enough to reconsider every life choice involving cardio. "What's wrong?"

Crystal was standing beside the bed, holding up the fitted sheet we'd slept on.

*No fire. No burglar. No blood. No spider.*

From what I could see, she was perfectly fine. Not to complain, but her shriek really oversold this whole thing. My adrenaline was still surging when she spoke up.

"Yeah, look at this."

I stepped closer.

*What exactly am I ...*

There it was near the bottom of the sheet. A hole. Not an "oops, I snagged it on something" hole, but a crater the size of a large grapefruit.

I leaned in, touched the shredded fabric, and examined the ragged edges.

*Teeth marks.*

For a beat, neither of us said anything.

Then Crystal snorted.

I tried to hold it together. I really did.

But then she started laughing—that kind where her eyes squeezed shut and her shoulders shook. No sound came out at first, as if she couldn't get enough air to make it loud. Then she doubled over, finally squealing, still clutching the sheet in her hands. I'll never forget that sound.

I braced myself against the dresser as tears formed in my eyes for the second time in twelve hours, though for a very different reason. At some point, I'd stopped laughing at the hole and was laughing at her laugh.

"We slept on this!" she gasped between breaths. "On this hole."

"I know."

She tried to compose herself, failed, then said, "A hole."

I laughed harder. "Okay, stop saying 'hole.'"

*We aren't twelve.*

"Why? What's wrong with hole?"

*Apparently we are.*

A slow grin spread across her face. "Wait ... holy sheet."

I smirked.

She stretched it out this time, undeniably delighted with herself. "Holy sheeet. You know ... like holy sh—"

*No mileage left on that one.*

I cackled. "No, no, say it again. Maybe I'll get it this time."

She swatted at me. "Oh, whatever."

Pattering paws on the floor made us both turn. The boys came barreling down the hall, springing onto the bed—Max first, then Spartacus—and rolling on the bare mattress with a conviction that said their kennel Exodus was over and they'd finally reached the Promised Land.

(Someone cue the angelic choir and drop a beam of light from the heavens.)

Crystal held up the ruined sheet. "Okay, who did this?"

The rolling stopped. Two heads popped up. Four ears perked.

I pointed at Max. "Was it you, naughty doggy?"

He turned his head to the side but kept his eyes on me, as if maybe that would somehow make him invisible.

"Or you?" Crystal pointed at Spartacus.

He sat up a little straighter, clearly trying to look like the more responsible sibling.

Then, as if this had never happened, they both went back to tumbling across the mattress in a blur of black and white. Max leaped, pinning Spartacus for a half-second before Spartacus rolled free with a burst of surprising force. They slid across the mattress, scrabbling for traction as pillows toppled to the floor.

Crystal looked at me. "Think we'll ever find out who did it?"

"Nope."

She sighed and tossed the sheet onto the floor. "Just this once, huh?"

I smiled. "Yeah. Just this once."

*"Just watching my daddy type."*

*"Okay bro, let me tell you how I broke out of my kennel ..."*

# 11

# Grown, Not Born

TODAY HAD BEEN MISERABLY slow. I took my break later than usual and opened my inbox with the kind of hope a person has right before checking their credit card statement.

*Please, no surprises.*

The first email was a scheduling request. Someone needed next Saturday off for a "family emergency," which you never really knew if it were true. In this case, they must've forgotten we were friends on Facebook, because I'd already seen their post about going to the UGA game that day.

I hit *Approve* anyway, partly because we could make it work and they'd covered shifts for us when we were in a jam. There was also a piece of me that admired the courage it took to lie to your boss when what you really needed was simply a day to go be happy somewhere else. If giving them that made their week better, it felt worth it.

Next was a vendor confirmation. I skimmed the invoice, tapped *Approve*, and moved on.

Then I opened a message from corporate with the cheerful subject line: *NEW ICE CREAM MACHINE CLEANING METHODS!*

*Yay!*

The diagrams showed tubes, gaskets, and O-rings arranged in the exact current set up—just now with extra steps guaranteed to slow us down. Arrows and bold text insisted it was "more efficient," which felt like Corporate patting us on the head and saying, "Good luck."

I rubbed my forehead.

*Great.*

Another announcement they'd expect *me* to deliver with a smile.

I marked it as read and dragged it into the *Later* folder. I breezed through the rest of the emails, answered what I could, flagged the rest, and kept going.

Then I switched to my Lexi's Legacy account. The inbox was fuller than I'd expected. I scrolled past a couple of donation receipts, read a follow-up from a meeting I hardly remembered, and answered a message from a rescue in Tennessee asking for help with an intake. Then—

My thumb hovered.

A notification from Bank of America.

My stomach dipped.

*Did I overdraft?*

I sat up straighter and tapped it open.

The first line appeared: *We are pleased to inform you that your grant application has been approved.*

I exhaled, hard.

It wasn't a monumental amount, but it was enough to cover supplies for two shelters through the end of the quarter. There'd be some happy animals this winter, and that thought put a smile on my face.

With a few minutes left on my break, I closed my email and opened Instagram. My feed filled instantly with rescue posts: A senior Lab padding out the door with his new family. A military vet reunited with his cat after deployment. A horse sanctuary showed off a birthday cake made of hay and carrots for their newest rescue.

I kept scrolling. Then I stopped.

A video auto-played before I could take my eyes off it.

A dark concrete room. Metal grates. Piglets—pink, trembling, huddled together.

They were the same size as *Max.* The same size as *Spartacus.*

The sound hit first—screaming.

High-pitched, frantic, and *unmistakably* afraid.

Then the image: a worker.

A hammer.

The swing.

The impact.

More screaming.

Then one broke free—

Running, slipping, and desperate for any way out.

The piglet crashed into the wall and spun back, trapped in a corner.

The worker stepped forward, cutting off any escape.

He raised the hammer.

And—

I swiped away so fast I nearly dropped my phone. My hands shook. I locked the screen and shoved it into my pocket. For a full minute, I just sat there staring at nothing. Then I stood, cleared my tray, and went back to work.

Back at the bagging area, I fell into the same motions I'd done a thousand times before.

*Check the bag.*

*Hand it off.*

*Next order.*

A team member slid a sandwich through the chute. "Extra bacon, extra cheese, extra pickles." I reached for it. A strip of bacon poked from under the edge of the wrapper—only slightly, the way it did whenever sandwiches were overloaded. I went to tuck it back in, pressing the foil tighter, and felt it snap beneath my fingers.

My stomach turned.

I placed the sandwich in the bag, folded the top, and handed it to the team member at the window. "Here."

Dryness climbed up my throat.

*Need water.*

I stepped to the back, and as I passed the grill station, the heat rolled over me. Chicken breasts hissed and popped in neat rows. The smell of cooking meat filled the air; I'd grown so used to it that it barely registered anymore.

"You okay, man?" Gary appeared beside me. "You look out of it."

"I'm fine." I kept going. "Just tired."

He nodded, satisfied enough, and moved on.

The shift crawled forward. With every sandwich I saw, every order I called, every time I caught a glimpse of the menu board, something inside me flinched.

By the time I clocked out, I felt like I'd worked a double.

In the car, I didn't start the engine right away.

The parking lot was half-lit. Headlights swept across the asphalt as cars pulled in and out. I sat there with my hands on the wheel, staring out the windshield. A family crossed in front of me, bags of food swinging at their sides. One kid tore open his box before they even reached their car.

The video replayed in my mind—images, sounds, all of it. I pressed fingers against my temples.

*What am I doing?*

I ran a nonprofit dedicated to saving dogs and cats. I spent my nights and weekends raising money for rescues and advocating for creatures who couldn't speak for themselves. That was my mission. That was my purpose.

Somewhere along the way, I'd gotten good at living in two different worlds.

I'd see the commercials—the ones with the happy cows grazing in fields, the soft music playing in the background, the promise of humane treatment—and I never questioned it.

But seeing it on video—seeing the fear, hearing the screams, the reality—was different. It was nothing like the commercials and certainly nothing like the sanitized marketing language people used:

*Ethically sourced.*

*Free-range.*

*Humane slaughter.*

Saying those words side by side—humane *and* slaughter—made no sense at all.

*How do you humanely slaughter anyone?*

It felt like I'd been lied to. Or maybe I'd just lied to myself.

For years, I'd come here, day in and day out, and sold products that existed because animals had suffered horrendously and lost their lives over a sandwich.

I'd never let myself look at it directly. It had always been easier not to. But now I felt awake.

The moment I walked through the front door, Max and Spartacus were on me. I crouched, and for a moment, I stayed there, one hand on Max's back, the other scratching Spartacus's.

Crystal came out of the kitchen, drying her hands on a towel. "Hey. How was—" She stopped. "You okay?"

She always knew when something was wrong.

I opened my mouth to answer, but whatever I meant to say didn't make it out. I pushed myself up slowly. Then, something in my throat tightened and loosened all at once. "I just can't ..."

"Can't what?" she asked gently.

The words slipped out before I had time to second-guess them. "I'm ... going vegan."

A breath passed.

Crystal blinked. "You're ... what?"

"Vegan. I'm going vegan. Tonight. Like right now."

She looked at me as if I'd just announced we were moving to Antarctica tomorrow.

I walked past her into the living room and sank onto the couch. Max jumped up beside me. Spartacus followed, settling on the other side. Crystal sat across from me and leaned in.

"I saw something today," I said. "A video. On Instagram." I paused, trying to find the words. "It was a slaughterhouse. Piglets. They were—"

She scooted closer.

"And I know we all know this, right? We know where meat comes from. We know what happens. But I've never let myself *really* think about it." I looked down at Max, who was watching me. "If someone did to them what happens to those animals every single day—" My voice buckled. "It'd be a crime."

Silence settled between us.

Crystal nodded slowly, seeming to absorb everything. "Okay," she finally said.

A strange thing tugged at my chest—not the fear of changing my life, but the realization that I'd been nervous to tell her at all. She'd never given me a reason to be. I could tell her anything, and it would always be okay.

"Okay, what?" I asked.

She placed her hand on my arm. "If this is what you need to do, then we'll figure it out. I'll look up some vegan recipes."

A month later, I'd learned one undeniable truth about veganism:

Powdered milk was in *everything*.

Soups, condiments, chips. You name it. If an ingredient list existed, powdered milk had probably found a way onto it.

One evening—before I'd become that person in the grocery store, squinting at labels—Crystal had made these meatless pot pies I was excited about. The box practically screamed 100% vegan, so I didn't think twice. After dinner, I flipped the box over to check the calories, and there it was, halfway down the ingredient list: *Whey.*

"You're kidding," I muttered, holding it up for Crystal to see.

She winced. "Oh ..."

The same thing happened with gummy bears soon after. I'd been so proud of myself for finding a "fruit" snack ... right until I learned what gelatin actually was.

At first, I beat myself up way more than the mistake deserved. But eventually, I realized something: I wasn't perfect, but I was trying. Learning. Adjusting.

And that had to count for something.

At work, the questions had started almost immediately.

"You're not eating chicken anymore?" Haley had asked during a break. "You work at Chick-fil-A."

"I know where I work."

"So what do you eat here?"

"Fruit cups. Waffle fries. Side salads. Polynesian sauce too." I shrugged. "It's not ideal."

Some people got it. They'd nod, ask a few questions, and move on. Others stared like I'd joined some new-age cult and was about to hand them a pamphlet.

"But bacon though," one of the kitchen guys had said, shaking his head. "I could never give it up."

That "it" had been *someone*, not something.

Still, I didn't push. I'd been alive long enough to know that doing so only made people defensive. So I answered only when asked, explained when it felt right, and kept my head down the rest of the time.

An employee anniversary celebration was held on a Saturday afternoon. The break room had been decorated with streamers, a balloon, a banner, and there was a spread of food on the folding tables.

I stood near the back with a cup of lemonade, trying to look appropriately festive.

The operator's wife approached with a paper plate. On it sat a thick slice of homemade chocolate cake with frosting piped in neat little ridges. She'd made it herself.

"Kerk!" She handed me a plate. "Here ya go."

My eyes moved from the cake to her hopeful smile. I hated to ruin the moment—she'd clearly put love into it. "Looks great, but I can't. I'm vegan."

Her smile flickered, and she pulled the plate back. "Oh! When did that happen?"

"About a month ago."

"Wow." She tilted her head. "What made you choose that?"

*Hmmm ...*

How do you explain a slaughterhouse video while standing in a decorated break room filled with party favors and bright colors?

How do you describe the sound that won't leave your head, or the way you can't look at a menu the same way anymore?

How do you explain the weight of realizing your *entire* career is built on something you can no longer justify?

You don't. Not here, anyway.

"I just ..."

She glanced over my shoulder and gave a polite smile to someone behind me.

"I just prefer my food to be grown," I said finally, "not born."

She nodded slowly, the way people do when they don't really understand but don't want to say so.

From across the room, my operator's voice cut through the noise. "Careful, honey. Kerk here is saving the animals now." He chuckled, lifting his cup in a mock toast.

A few people laughed.

*What's so funny about compassion for all animals?*

My mind flashed back to the time on the bus in middle school, when some older kid decided my at-home haircut looked "gay" and everyone else agreed.

My face went hot.

My ears rang.

I couldn't tell if people were still looking at me or if it just felt like they were, so I forced a thin smile. "Someone's gotta do it."

*Running.*
   *Dark tunnel.*
   *Footsteps slamming the ground behind me.*
   *A figure I can't see, only feel—close, too close.*
   *My legs are heavy. Not moving fast enough.*
   *I stumble.*
   *The shadow lunges—*

I jolted awake, heart pounding and sweat on my forehead.

Darkness.

Red glowing light. Alarm clock.

*My room.*

A warm weight on my chest.

*Max?*

A wet tongue dragged across my cheek.

"Hey boy," I whispered.

I turned my head. Crystal was asleep beside me. At her
legs, Spartacus was curled, snoring. I let out a slow breath
and sank into the pillow. Max nudged closer, fitting himself into the curve of my arm.

It had been a week since the break-room incident and a
week since the truth finally settled into my bones:

*I don't belong there anymore.*

The thought had been lingering, and every day I walked
into that building, I felt like I was drowning in slow motion. I knew what I needed to do. Still, the practical voice
nagged:

*The mortgage. The bills.*

*No other job lined up.*

*Crystal and the boys depend on me.*

*NO safety net.*

Each thought piled on the next until I felt wetness on
my face.

Maybe I could just stay—keep cashing the checks and
pretend the contradiction wasn't there. People did it every
day. I'd done it too.

The thought dimmed something in me.

I squeezed my eyes shut and pulled Max a little closer; 6:00 a.m. would be here soon.

*A city award for our work at Chick-fil-A.*
*Grateful to have worked with my love.*

*A vegan dessert dish by the super talented Crystal.*

*"What's Mom cooking for us?"*

*A new friend at Sleepy Pig Farm Sanctuary.*

*Hanging out with little Sparky.*

*New friends at Old Fogey Farm Sanctuary.*

# 12

# A New World

**Year Four**

**2021**

"Alright, boys," I said, dragging the box over the carpet.

Max trotted closer while Spartacus trailed.

I reached for the scissors on my desk ...

*Where'd they go?*

I nudged my Julius Caesar penholder. Something peeked out from under the papers.

Not the scissors.

*That GameStop gift card.*

I flipped it over.

*$100.*

I'd forgotten I even had it, and I'd literally just bought a Nintendo Switch a few weeks earlier.

*Of course.*

Alanis Morissette's *Ironic* played in my head as I moved the card aside and kept searching. I checked the desk drawers. Then the shelf.

Nothing.

I looked to the boys. "Stay here."

Max immediately planted his paws on the box. Spartacus sniffed at the corners.

"Boys, it's not food. Chill."

Even if it were food, does Max honestly think at this point I'd ever leave it unguarded around him?

I jogged to the kitchen and grabbed one of Crystal's good knives—a choice she absolutely would not have approved of—then hurried back before either dog tried to chew it open.

I slid the blade through the tape; the flaps popped open. But before I let myself look inside, I carried the knife back to the kitchen. I washed it, dried it, and placed it back into the block.

*She'll never know.*

When I returned, Max practically had his entire head inside the box; only his back paws and tail were visible. Spartacus lingered nearby, close enough to monitor the situation, but far enough to claim, "I'm just a bystander."

"That's a no-no, Max," I said, scooping him up.

He squirmed and flashed the tiniest bit of teeth, letting out a dramatic growl.

I fought a grin. "Don't growl at your daddy."

Max delivered a perfect side-eye as I set him down. Spartacus glanced over at him with the quiet judgment of a brother who'd seen this show before.

When I finally leaned over the box, I pulled the flaps back even farther. A wad of brown, crinkled paper puffed up. I grabbed it, tossed it behind me, and crouched to get a closer look.

Something caught the light.

Right on top lay rows of the same image—Spartacus's face front and center, tongue lolling under a stretch of blue skies. My hand paused above the stack before I touched the top one. The matte finish felt velvety. I eased my fingers underneath and lifted. The bold lettering came into focus as I tilted it.

***Pawprints on Our Hearts.***

Awe settled over me.

*My book.*

Written right here in this room—beside my boys—on nights I wasn't sure I had anything left to give.

I held the book low so they could see it. "We did it, boys."

Max stepped back, grabbed his toy, marched over to the box of my author copies, and dropped it. Spartacus stared just enough to verify that he was, in fact, the dog on the cover.

By lunchtime, the pizza had already arrived. Papa John's was my go-to celebration meal. I'd figured out how to make it vegan: no cheese, no extras, and sauce. It was basically a glorified piece of toast. Still great though.

I've always loved pizza—hot, cold, day-old, whatever form it took. In college, my buddy Drew and I attempted the *Goliath Challenge*—a monstrous pizza meant for *three* people to finish in under an hour without standing. Few ever had. Winners didn't have to pay for the $80.00 pizza and got *free* T-shirts, which, for broke college students, felt like winning the lottery.

We didn't bother finding a third. We figured, *how hard can it be? Two's plenty.*

Leading up to it, we "trained" by chugging obscene amounts of water and stuffing ourselves to stretch our stomachs like competitive eaters. When the big day came, we powered through—sweating, of course—until the final two slices. That was it. I stumbled outside and threw up behind the restaurant.

As I wiped my mouth, I looked at Drew. "Dude, we should've gotten a third."

Naturally, I went out that night, drank too much cheap tequila, and crashed at home. The next morning, I woke up starving, saw a slice of pizza my roommate had left on the counter—at least fourteen hours old—and ate it straight from the open box. My stomach didn't even flinch.

So yeah, pizza and I had been through the good, the bad, and the ugly. And today was definitely one of the good ones.

I eased onto the couch, balancing the plate on my knee. Spartacus sprawled on the rug, head resting on his paws. I patted the cushion directly in front of me so Max would sit where I could keep an eye on him, ever since *Pizza Gate*. On that particular night, a friend had set her plate on the counter. Max leaped, grabbed it, and tore through the house, finishing the slice *mid-run*.

*Lesson learned.*

I pointed. "Max, sit."

Max hopped onto the cushion and sat facing forward like a perfect little angel. Except every few seconds, he'd slowly turn his head with a sly side-eye. The moment we made eye contact, he snapped his gaze forward again, sitting taller.

Then again. And again.

By the fourth time, he realized I was watching his every move. He let out a huff and stayed put.

I smiled. "See, you can be a good boy when you wanna be."

Once I knew for certain that Max's attention was away from my plate, I relaxed and focused on the American Revolution series playing on PBS.

Lunch breaks had become a sacred ritual since leaving Chick-fil-A earlier in the year. No phone or checking messages on the laptop; only food, my boys, and whatever we were watching.

But today was release day.

*Just one peek.*

I hurried through the last bite and set the empty plate on the coffee table. Max leaned forward, sniffing at it with a level of heartbreak unmerited for the situation. When he confirmed there wasn't even a crumb, he sat back with a resigned sigh.

I broke my own rule and reached for my phone. The screen lit up, and I swiped open my sales dashboard first.

*Whoa! Is this right?*

My heart thudded.

I tapped over to my Amazon book page, then refreshed it.

The screen reloaded—and there it was.

I blinked and held the phone closer to my face.

The orange banner: *#1 Best Seller.*

I refreshed again to make sure my eyes weren't messing with me.

*Still there.*

Then I checked Amazon UK: *Best Seller.*

Then Amazon Australia: *Best Seller.*

Then Amazon Canada: *Best Seller.*

I sank back and exhaled. "International bestseller."

What a weird thing to say.

*Me?*

What a weird thing to even think.

I scrolled and clicked on the category page that showed what customers in *Coming-of-Age Memoirs* were buying. And sitting right next to *Pawprints On Our Hearts*, was Matthew McConaughey's *Greenlights*.

I laughed out loud.

*Unreal.*

But it was. The banners were right there, and strangers in countries I'd never visited were buying a book I wrote between Chick-fil-A shifts and late nights on a futon.

I sat there, letting myself take it all in.

Max and Spartacus started wrestling on the floor, rolling around and into each other like tiny tumbleweeds. They'd been with me through every word I'd written, every single scene, and every late-night where I'd doubted myself. Watching them now, lost in play and completely oblivious to the moment happening above them, made the whole thing feel bigger than just some book. It felt as if a piece of my life had finally landed where it belonged.

My eyes drifted to the wall—Lexi's pink bandana hanging from its hook, and next to it, the photo of me and Gunner. I gazed at them with a sort of reverence, and the room seemed to grow quiet around me. This moment belonged to them, too. The book existed because of *them*.

Once, this all had felt impossible. There'd been a time when the idea of writing a book was something only other people did. Not people like me.

I exhaled—slowly and full.

And then, for reasons I couldn't quite explain, my old boss's face surfaced. I remembered how he'd looked at me when I told him about my writing venture, like I wasn't competent enough to write anything more than a schedule.

Before I could stop it, my mind slipped back to the last conversation we ever had...

On the walk to the operator's office, I rehearsed what I'd say. I'd done it in the shower many times before. The lines felt simple enough in my head, almost routine by then. I stepped inside and sat across from him. When I tried running through the lines again, one last time, they scattered the moment he looked at me.

"So." He leaned back in his chair. "What's on your mind?"

I folded my hands in my lap and opened my mouth. "I'm …"

Nothing else came out.

A light sway passed through my head, like I'd stood up too fast. Except I hadn't moved.

"Kerk?"

He sounded far away.

"Kerk."

The second time sounded clearer.

*Just keep it simple.*

I breathed in, then out. "I'm leaving."

The words hung there. He studied me with a measuring look. "Leaving?"

"Yes, sir."

He blinked once. "For another company?"

"No."

A beat passed.

"Then … where?"

"Nowhere." I swallowed. "Just … not here."

He squinted, and his eyebrows pinched.

I sat a little straighter. "It's ... about my convictions. I've been thinking about what I believe. About the food industry and—" I paused, searching for words that didn't sound preachy. "I can't work in a place that conflicts with my values anymore."

*I actually did it.*

His mouth curved into something that was almost a smile. Then he chuckled, throwing his hands up. "So what, you're going to go save the chickens now?"

Heat rose in my face. "Something like that."

He just shook his head.

I thought that was the end of it. All that was left was to work out my notice and move on.

Then he leaned forward, fingers steepled on the desk. "We need to make a video."

"A video?"

"For the team. To explain why you're leaving." He said it like it was the most obvious thing in the world. "We need to get ahead of this."

"Okayyy." I dragged it out. "What am I supposed to say?" I'd never had to do a goodbye video for any company I'd worked for.

"We'll say you're leaving to focus on your nonprofit. The animal rescue thing." He waved his hand. "People can understand that."

A knot formed in my stomach. "But that's not why I'm leaving."

"Excuse me?"

"The nonprofit is part of it, sure. But that's not why." I looked him dead in the eye. "I just told you *the* reason: my convictions. I don't feel comfortable being part of this industry anymore. I don't feel right asking people to—"

"We're not telling them that."

"What are you talking about?"

"You're the freakin' executive director. We're not going to stand up there and let you tell everyone you're leaving because you think we're doing the wrong thing." His voice grew sharper. "That's not the message we're sending."

"I don't feel like the experience we give our customers and the community is wrong. I feel like the—"

"Stop!"

The bluntness stunned me. Still, I managed to speak up. "I've worked with these people for years. They deserve to know—"

"They deserve to know what we tell them."

"I'm not comfortable lying to—"

"We're doing it my way, or I'll get legal involved."

I felt the blood drain from my face.

*Legal? For telling the truth?*

*Can they actually do anything?*

My mind jumped to the employee agreement I'd signed years ago.

*Did it say anything about—*

"Do we have an understanding?"

I wanted to tell him exactly what I thought. I wanted to walk out and defend my truth. But I had Crystal and the boys. A life that depended on me not making enemies

on my way out the door. So, I said the only thing I could.
"Fine."

He nodded. "Good. We'll record next week."

I stood and left without another word.

*WHAM!*

Sixteen pounds of Yorkipoo slammed into my sternum.
*What the h—*

The air left my lungs as I tipped over just in time to
see Max ricochet off me at a sideways angle. He launched
toward the far end of the couch, skidded, pivoted, and
bolted for the kitchen in a frantic blur of black.

Spartacus trailed him, though he didn't seem entirely
sure of what game they were playing.

By the time I made it to my feet, Max was already scanning every surface for potential snacks. "Maximus!"

He barely glanced back.

I waved a finger. "You know that's a no-no."

My phone alarm chimed.

*Can't be late.*

"Come on, boys. Let's hang out."

At *hang,* Max's tail flicked—then he rocketed toward
the office.

Spartacus and I followed.

The Zoom call connected, and a woman's nervous smile filled my screen, framed by a backdrop of color-coordinated books and a few plants. "Hey, Kerk!" she said with a small wave. "I'm so excited to finally meet you."

"Nice to meet you, Bridget." I clicked her file open on my second monitor. "I looked over your outline. You did a great job. Very well thought out."

Her whole face brightened. "Really?"

"Yes, really." I smiled, leaning in.

"It's just ..." She tucked a strand of hair behind her ear. "I've never written a book before. I don't know if anyone would even read it."

"Let me tell you something." I folded my arms and met her gaze. "I felt exactly the same when I wrote mine. The people who need it are out there. Our job is just to get it to them."

We spent the next hour discussing how to turn her outline into scenes and chapters. By the end of the session, she was glowing.

"Thanks so much," she said. "I feel like I can actually do this."

"You can. I'll talk to you next week."

The call ended, and I sat back in my chair. Some days, I still couldn't believe this was my job now. The company had hired me the same week I'd quit Chick-fil-A. No gap in income. I'd jumped, and the safety net had shown up.

After the way I'd been treated by our operator, Crystal decided she was done too, and quit on the same day I had. She landed a job at a medical office not long after, and for the first time in years, she came home smiling instead of drained.

My new role was teaching authors how to write and publish their books. Most days I was on calls like the one with Bridget; on other days, I coached the coaches, built systems, and celebrated their wins. Sometimes I even wore pajama bottoms with only my "professional" shirt visible on camera. And I got paid to do it from this room, sitting right here in this chair. I'd never had a fully remote job before. When I first started, I wasn't sure I'd adjust.

Turns out I loved it.

I was saving hours every week that used to get eaten by the commute. No more packing lunches in Tupperware or working twelve-hour shifts on floors that hurt my feet. Rolling out of bed and being at work in seven minutes flat felt like winning the lottery.

Throughout my workday, I often thought about who I'd been a year earlier. If you'd told me I'd start an animal-advocacy nonprofit, write a bestseller, go vegan, and leave my career at Chick-fil-A, I would've laughed and said you had the wrong guy.

But here I was. And maybe that's the thing about life; if we're willing to let go of who we are, one day, we'll arrive at who we're meant to be.

As I let the thought settle, Max appeared in the doorway. He paused, assessing whether anything interesting was happening. Spartacus, who'd been asleep in the corner beside the bookshelf, lifted his head but didn't move.

I looked at Max. "Just working, boy."

Max trotted out and returned seconds later with one of his toys, dropping it beneath my chair.

I checked the clock.

*An hour until my next call.*

I smiled. "Okay, boys. Let's go."

When we stepped outside into the late-morning light, a breeze drifted by, carrying the sweet scent of honeysuckle layered with the warm, earthy smell of the ground. Across the way, the neighbor's laundry swayed on the line. Above us, two small birds called back and forth, swooping through the branches.

Max trotted ahead into the grass, nose down, tail wagging with that certain rhythm that meant he'd found something worth inspecting. Spartacus stretched—back arched, paws spread—then gave a shake that sent his ears flapping before he bounded after his brother. They moved through the yard how they always did, weaving around each other and stopping at a certain patch of grass. Max lifted his leg first, claiming the spot. Spartacus followed, sniffing, considering, then added his own contribution.

A moment later, Max went to the same spot and peed again. Spartacus bumped him with a playful nip, then darted away. Max chased after him, and the two zigzagged through the grass in a scene that could only be summed up by Fyodor Dostoevsky's words: *joy untroubled.*

I smiled, soaking it all in—middle of the workday, sunlight on my face, and taking a break because I *could*, not because someone had finally approved one.

*Strange.*

Even though it had been nearly a year since I'd left Chick-fil-A, moments like this still felt new.

I reached into the basket beside the door and grabbed a tennis ball. I bounced it once on the concrete and caught it. That single *thup* was all it took for both boys to snap to attention. They barked wildly as they sprinted back and skidded to a stop at the edge of the grass.

They knew this game.

I bounced the ball again, harder this time. It shot up, smacked the roof, and ricocheted into the yard. Grass and dirt flew beneath the rush of their paws. I shaded my eyes, trying to track the two streaks of black and white flying across the lawn. Both dogs vanished behind the bushes, leaving me with only the sun's glare.

I waited.

A car door slammed somewhere down the block, followed by distant voices floating over the fence. Someone laughed.

Then came a rustle of leaves, a bark, and the telltale *jingle-jangle* of tags racing my way.

I squinted toward the sound, and Max burst back into view with the ball clamped between his teeth. Spartacus trailed him, not seeming the least bit upset. Probably because there'd be another round.

There was *always* another round now.

I grinned, took the ball, and bounced it again.

*"Just one bite. I won't tell Mom."*

*"My favorite toy!"*

*"Sometimes we like to tan after lunch."*

*"Are you gonna throw the ball or not?"*

*"Dad think's he's gonna get some work done. We'll see."*

# 13

# A Good Life

## Year Five

## 2022

I BARELY RECOGNIZED THE trees outside my window. The leaves that were once green had crisped into amber, then disappeared altogether. Within that slow shift of seasons, things had settled into a pleasant loop: Wake up. Breakfast. Calls. Lunch with the boys. More calls. Dinner. Repeat.

This was my life now. And it was a good life. I believed that.

Between calls, I opened my dashboard and scrolled through the numbers. *Pawprints on Our Hearts* had been out for over a year, and still the royalties surprised me. I'd been able to pour more into Lexi's Legacy than I'd ever thought possible. I clicked over to our monthly donation tracker.

*Forty-seven animals.*

Food, medical care, emergency rescues—all funded by people buying a book I'd written on a futon.

*And I almost gave up on page one.*

I leaned back in my chair and smiled.

Max wandered in from the hallway and plopped onto one of the dog beds by the bookshelf. Spartacus was already there, curled in his usual crescent position.

*Ping!*

A Slack notification from Brittany, one of the other coaches, popped up on my laptop: *Hey! Quick question. Can you hop on a call with Brenda tomorrow? She's struggling with her draft and specifically asked for you.*

I typed back: *Of course. Send me her file and I'll go over it tonight.*

I closed the message and stared at the screen. This job was good. Better than good, really. Much better than any job I'd ever had.

My phone buzzed with a text from my manager:

> Hey bro. I know you've got a lot on your plate, but is there any chance you can do Friday's webinar? Aaron's gonna be out.

Somehow, those had become *my* responsibility lately. A week earlier, I'd agreed to cover for someone else.

"Alright, everyone," I'd said, walking through the new product features and answering questions in the chat while trying to keep the pace light. After the pitch, I fielded objections and even helped close two new clients.

Normally, the sales team earned a bonus for that, but I wasn't in sales. Still, afterward, I'd sent a quick message to payroll: *Hey, should I expect the webinar bonus on this check or the next?*

The reply came two days later: *Webinars aren't included in your role's compensation structure.*

I tried not to let it bother me more than it needed to. Maybe this was just a onetime thing.

But here we were again.

I sat with it for a second. This job had taken a chance on me when I'd needed it. It was remote, my teammates were awesome, and overall, they treated me better than Chick-fil-A ever had. Heck, the company even covered two monthly hour-long massages as part of a self-care benefit. Hard to complain about that.

I typed back:

> *Sure, I can do it.*

I'd hardly lifted my thumb from the screen when his reply buzzed in: *You're a lifesaver!*

I set the phone down without responding and rubbed my temples. My thoughts slid back to our last leadership meeting, when the CEO had unveiled a new initiative: an extra check-in call with every client to "elevate the experience."

The Zoom squares flickered with polite smiles. I'd un-muted and asked how my team was supposed to fit another call into calendars already packed with coaching sessions and backend projects. Then I asked whether compensation or call-tracking procedures needed to be adjusted for my team to get credit for them.

There was a pause long enough to hear someone typing. Then the CEO gave his over-the-top cheery smile. "Books change lives. We get to build something our grandkids will be proud of."

As soon as he finished, a Slack notification blinked in the corner of my screen from another team lead: *Yup. Looks like we're not getting paid for this one either.*

A second message came before I could finish reading the first: *Sooo we get to lose a few hundred bucks a month while he sits at his six-million-dollar lake house, which is right across from Matthew McConaughey's? Cool cool. Can't wait to share the news.*

The room nodded in unison.

I nodded too, but not for the same reasons. I'd heard phrases like that before. Everywhere I'd ever worked, really. It always meant the same thing: *We need more from you, and though you won't be paid for it, we're hoping you won't notice.*

But I noticed.

Within me, a response came together in an instant, and I was one breath away from unmuting when something Benjamin Franklin once wrote flashed through my mind: *A slip of the foot you may soon recover, but a slip of the tongue you may never get over.*

My finger eased off the mouse. I stayed silent and let the moment pass.

A soft *thud* hit the carpet behind me, pulling me out of my thoughts. I glanced over my shoulder.

My display copy of *Pawprints on Our Hearts* lay on the floor.

And there was Max—front paws braced, hips rapid-firing into the dog bed, nudging it further into the bookshelf.

I put it all together quickly: Max had humped his bed so hard he'd knocked my book off the shelf.

"Maximus Murray, that's a no-no."

He froze and turned toward me. When I saw his face, a part of me felt wrong. I wouldn't want someone interrupting me—mid *you know what*—either. But still ... maybe don't do it right in front of your family, dude.

We held eye contact for a beat, both seeming unsure of what should happen next. Then, in one smooth motion, Max rolled onto his back and began sniffing himself.

Nearby, Spartacus cracked one eye open, then closed it again.

I felt the corners of my mouth lift and stretch into a smile.

*My boys.*

I walked over and grabbed Max's bed, dragging it back to its spot. It had shifted a good foot. When he saw me tugging it, he leaped onto it. He planted his paws, lifted his chest, and swished his tail wildly.

I chuckled. "Okay, boy."

I gave him one slow pull around the room, expecting him to hop off. Instead, Max leaned forward as if he were helping steer. The look on his face said the rest.

So, I circled the room again. Then again. By the fourth lap, he looked downright proud of himself. When I finally stopped, Max glared up at me like, "We're just getting to the good part."

I straightened the bed, smoothed the rumpled fabric, and gave him a pat. He didn't lean into it; he just gave me the side-eye. "Don't look at me like that, Max."

I turned away, and a low whine rose behind me, followed by the jingle of his tags as he strutted off down the hall.

*Drama king.*

A notification chimed from my computer, then chimed again a second later.

*Ugh. Leadership meeting soon.*

I glanced toward the computer, then dropped to one knee and scooped up the fallen book. I held it upright, and something about the cover made me pause. Maybe it was the glassy shine in Spartacus's eyes, or the way the light caught each tiny hair on his snout, or the grooves along his tongue. He looked so alive in that moment, it almost hurt.

I stood, and my eyes went to Spartacus, who was still snoozing away in his dog bed.

My mouth twitched, and a small warmth moved through me. It lingered as I flipped the pages. I landed on a photo of Lexi on my lap, taken a week or so after my senior prom.

*Almost twenty years ago.*

I was seventeen then—younger, thinner—sitting in the laundry room of my parents' house.

*Why didn't anyone tell me to get a haircut?*

We'd had spaghetti that night, and Lexi had tried to lick the sauce that had splattered across my favorite Abercrombie shirt. She'd gotten most of it.

At seventeen, my life had revolved around the most urgent, earth-shattering questions imaginable:

*Will I have time for Halo when I go off to college?*

*Does Mom know I snuck out last weekend?*

*Once I become a surgeon, what kind of Ferrari should I get?*

The thoughts pulled a grin out of me.

*Good times.*

The grin faded as I examined the photo more closely—the version of me trying to look older than he felt. He had no idea what was coming. And if I could go back and tell him everything that would happen, I wasn't sure he'd believe me.

I sighed and closed the book. It felt strange, holding all those years in my hands. I looked down at it again.

*What if I write another one?*

Not a memoir this time. Something different. Bigger, somehow.

*No, no, no. What if—*

The thought floated up, and I let it hang there.

*What if I wrote books for a living?*

I pictured it: no more Zoom calls on someone else's schedule. No more nodding along in meetings while some CEO talked about "building legacies" from a lake house I'd never be able to afford.

And beneath that image, more flashed: all the hours I'd poured in without being paid for them. Late nights answering messages no one else bothered to take. Covering for people when I was slammed with my own deadlines. Training new hires because I was "the best" with people.

I did more than my fair share because that's what the job needed ... except the job never paid more for needing more.

I'd spent my entire life building things that didn't belong to me—systems, teams, profits—and handing them over to people who received bonuses while I got the occasional "thank you," or pizza party or Starbucks gift card.

Writing professionally would be *my* hours, *my* voice, and *my* efforts building *my* dream instead of someone else's. It would all be mine.

The idea felt real in a way other dreams hadn't before; it was close enough to see, maybe even touch. Still, it was a big dream. There'd be so much to figure out. And ...

*I've only done one book. One.*

*What if it was a fluke?*

*What if readers hate the next one?*

*What if—*

My stomach tilted.

The edges of the room pressed in.

Another flutter came, sharper though.

The book slipped from my grip.

*Thud.*

I braced a hand against the wall and let myself sink down until I was sitting on the floor. The carpet was warm beneath my palms, and for a moment, I just closed my eyes.

*Maybe too big.*

*"If you wanna write books for a living, I know you can do it."*

*"Yeah, I believe in you too. Does this mean we'll get more snacks?"*

*"Will you have more time to take us to the beach again?"*

# 14

# The Last Straw

MAX HADN'T TOUCHED HIS breakfast.

Over the years, I'd never seen him turn down food. Not once. But this morning, he'd walked past his bowl, sniffed it, and kept going. Then, I followed him into the hallway, where he hunched over and threw up. By the time I reached him, he was trembling.

"It's okay, boy." I kneeled and placed my hand on his back. "Daddy's got you."

Crystal took him to the vet while I logged in for my first call. The diagnosis came via text an hour later:

> *Some stomach bug. Got meds. He's okay, just needs rest. Bringing him home now.*

When Crystal walked through the office door mid-call, she eased Max onto the floor. He didn't run to greet me like he usually did. He padded over slowly and tried to climb into my chair. I slid my arm beneath him and helped him up, and he curled into a tight ball against my chest, eyes half-closed.

"Hey, boy." I stroked his back gently. "You're gonna be okay."

He let out a small whine and pressed closer as if my presence could fix whatever was wrong.

I wished it worked that way.

The Zoom calls came one after another: a group call to review Amazon ads, a strategy call with a client whose launch had underperformed, and a coaching session on metadata optimization.

Throughout it all, Max stayed on my lap. He barely moved, just the occasional shift to find a more comfortable position or a slow blink when the calls first connected.

At some point, I pulled a second chair beside mine and draped a couple of blankets over it, in case Max wanted to sit near me and not on me. He never switched over.

Instead, Spartacus reared back and launched himself upward. His front paws caught the edge of the chair before he slid back down.

I muted myself, reached over, and placed him on the seat. "Be careful, boy."

He immediately went to work scratching at the blankets and shoving his nose underneath as if arranging them just right. Then he rolled onto his side with a small huff and settled in. From there, he faced us, and every so often, he peeked over to check on Max. Once he saw him, he'd close his eyes again.

Halfway through my 10:00 a.m. call, my client noticed him. "Max looks tired."

"Yeah, he's sick," I said, angling the camera so she could see him better.

"Poor baby." Her face softened. "Tell him I hope he feels better soon."

"I will."

By the third call, Max had become a recurring character. Every client who spotted him said something: "Give him pets for me," or "He's such a good boy," or "Let him rest, we can keep this short."

At noon, I joined the company-wide meeting.

*Forgot to grab lunch.*

I looked down at my lap. Max was snoring, still wrapped in the blanket I'd tucked around him after taking him and his brother out earlier.

I stayed put.

At least this was the one call where I didn't have to talk. I only had to listen while the CEO walked through slides about upcoming initiatives, new hires, and Q4 progress. I sat back and kept myself on mute.

In the middle of it, Max lifted his head, ears perking slightly, and came into view. For a moment, he studied the grid of faces on the screen. Then he sighed and lowered his head back onto my arm.

The chat lit up.

*OMG Max!*

*He's so precious.*

*MAXIMUS! MAXIMUS! Are you not entertained?*

I smiled at their enthusiasm.

The CEO wrapped things up, thanking everyone for their work before ending with our familiar sign-off. "Alright, everyone. Keep up the great work. And remember—books change lives."

The meeting ended, and my smile faded along with it.

Next up was my annual performance review with the CEO.

I wasn't dreading it exactly. I knew my numbers, and I'd exceeded every goal they'd set for me. I'd done everything they'd asked and then some.

Still, a part of me wished I could skip it or at least put it off until next week. I'd never left a one-on-one with him feeling better about anything.

I clicked the link anyway and waited for his face to appear.

"Kerk! Good to see you." His smile stretched wide. "Let's dive in."

He pulled up a document and shared his screen. My name sat at the top of a column of metrics.

"So." He leaned back. "You've had a fantastic year. Client satisfaction is up. Revenue contribution exceeded expectations. You built infrastructure the entire team is using now." He nodded. "Really strong results across the board."

I felt a small spark of satisfaction.

*Here comes my bonus!*

"Now," he said, moving to a new slide, "I do need to walk you through some changes we've made to our compensation structure."

The spark dimmed.

"We've restructured our incentive plan to better align with company goals moving forward. The old bonus tiers have been retired."

*Retired?*

"Under the previous structure, you would have qualified for a bonus this cycle."

*Would have?*

"But since we've transitioned to the new model, that bonus won't be paid out."

*What?!*

"I know that might be disappointing, but I'm confident you'll thrive under the new structure. This is really designed to reward top performers like yourself."

He clicked again. A chart appeared, filled with bars and percentages climbing upward. "To hit the first bonus tier, you'll need to help your clients publish at least forty books per quarter. Tier two is sixty. Top tier is eighty-five."

I ran the numbers in my head before I could stop myself.

*Forty books. Per quarter?*

This year, my best quarter had been nineteen. And that had nearly killed me.

"And to support our projected growth," he continued, clicking to another slide, "each coach will be onboarding sixty to eighty new clients per quarter."

I almost laughed.

"We're really excited about the scalability here," he said.

Scalability was a fun word for "we're going to squeeze as much out of you as we can."

"We think these targets will really push the team to the next level."

*Push them off a cliff, maybe.*

Unless I somehow tripled my results, I'd make less money.

"I really think next year is going to be your year," he said, smiling like he'd just handed me a gift.

Max shifted on my lap, and his head poked into the frame.

The CEO's expression changed. The warmth drained out of it. "Kerk, you shouldn't have your dog on camera during meetings."

"I know, it's just—"

"I saw him during the company meeting earlier too. You know our rules about that."

"He's sick and—"

"Don't do it again."

A brief silence fell between us, and the call ended.

I sat there staring at the empty screen.

I thought about the hours I'd poured into this job. The targets I'd hit. The systems I'd built from nothing so other people could do their jobs better. I thought about every time I'd said yes when I should've said no, every late night, every covered shift, every webinar I didn't get paid for.

And all that for a promise of "next year," an impossible workload, and a lecture about my sick dog.

I looked down as Max moved and gazed up at me with his heavy dark eyes. I rested my hand on his side and felt his ribs rise and fall beneath my palm.

Something was happening inside me, though I couldn't tell you what. I just knew what I needed to do.

*"Not feeling good so Mom took me to the vet. Waiting my turn."*

*"Daddy pays us in snacks for helping with his work."*

*"Long day at the office. Don't bother me."*

## 15

# Down the Rabbit Hole

**Year Six**

**2023**

OVER THE PAST FEW months, I'd devoured every animal book I could find—memoirs about dogs, novels told from a pet's perspective, and stories where animals saved their owners or the other way around. I read during lunch breaks, before bed, and sometimes in bed.

Some of them wrecked me. I'd finish a chapter and look at Max, who was inevitably watching, and I'd have to set the book aside just to breathe.

*How do people write things this beautiful?*

These authors knew what they were doing. They'd mastered something I was only beginning to understand.

Their prose flowed in ways mine never had, and their stories hit emotional beats I wasn't sure I could ever produce.

One late night, after finishing one, I closed the app on my phone and rubbed my eyes. The sheets were warm, and the sound machine had gone quiet at some point.

*Probably needs new batteries.*

Next to me, Crystal was already asleep. Max rolled against my side, settling deeper into my arm. Getting up didn't feel worth it now.

I gave him a small squeeze. "I don't know what story to write next, boy."

He cracked an eye open, yawned, then drifted off again.

*Thanks for the reassurance.*

Discovering the business side of authoring made it all worse. When I dug into industry data, the publishing landscape, and research into who actually made money as an author, I wasn't exactly encouraged.

The novels I admired in the animal genre—fiction and nonfiction—were all traditionally published with Big Five deals and film adaptations like *The Art of Racing in the Rain, Marley & Me,* and *A Dog's Journey.*

These authors had agents, marketing teams, and years of built-in readership.

How was I supposed to compete with that?

The indie publishing world had worked for *Pawprints On Our Hearts.* But making a full-time living from books required a whole other strategy. I'd need to build a cata-log, find readers, and somehow convince people to take a chance on an unknown author.

A few weeks later, I flew to my first author conference in Texas.

I didn't know what to expect. Part of me imagined a room full of people in tweed jackets debating the proper use of commas. What I found instead was a convention center packed with writers from every walk of life trying to figure out how to make this career work.

I attended panels on marketing, craft, and something called "reader magnets" that I pretended to understand. I took notes until my hand cramped and asked questions that probably revealed how little I knew.

I almost skipped the last session of the day. My feet hurt, my notebook was nearly full, and the coffee had stopped working hours ago.

But I stayed.

The speaker was a romance author. She clicked to a slide showing her income over the past ten years. The numbers climbed steadily—then sharply—until they hit a figure that made me sit up straighter.

I blinked, then read it again.

*From romance novels?*

She shared her process, her release schedule, and how she got her readers to devour everything she wrote. She spoke passionately about community, about connection, and about how romance readers felt like the most loyal fans in publishing.

I sat there absentmindedly chewing on the pen cap. *Romance.*

I'd never read a romance novel in my entire life. The closest I'd come was watching *The Last Song* with Crystal, which, fine, I teared up multiple times. And maybe I'd gotten a little too invested in Lorelai and Luke's situationship on *Gilmore Girls*. And okay, there was that weekend I watched *Sweet Home Alabama.* Twice.

Back home for weeks, I went down the rabbit hole.

Max and Spartacus were with me for all of it—wrestling around the room, then collapsing into naps on every possible spot, including beneath my desk. Sometimes Max would leap onto my lap and nudge my hand away from the keyboard. Even Spartacus would stretch out across my feet, as if to say, "Come on. Let's play."

My co-authors didn't help me with a single piece of research. But in their own way, they kept me grounded, reminding me why I was doing this at all, and that mattered just as much.

In between those moments, what I discovered surprised me. The romance genre was vast and wildly diverse. On one end, there was erotica that made me blush just reading the descriptions. And then, on the other, there were clean romances that felt like Hallmark movies in book form.

Every day after work, I kept digging.

Subgenres branched out into more subgenres. Small-town romance. Second-chance romance. Friends-to-lovers. Enemies-to-lovers. Grumpy-sunshine. There were cowboys, billionaires, and single dads. There were Christmas romances, beach romances, and romances set in bakeries, bookstores, and bed-and-breakfasts.

My head spun.

*How do people keep track of all this?*

One evening, Crystal appeared in the doorway. "How are my boys doing?"

"Good. Just researching."

"Sure." She smirked. "You've got that look."

"What look?"

"The same one you had before you left Chick-fil-A."

I chuckled.

"Don't stay up too late."

"I won't."

I decided to finish up the night by reading a few samples. Some were too spicy for my taste. Others felt too formulaic. And then I stumbled upon a book called *The Island House* by Elana Johnson.

I downloaded it, and four hours later, I finally looked up from my phone.

*This is it.*

The story was clean, heartfelt, and hopeful, with no explicit scenes. It had all the warmth and emotion of the movies I'd always loved.

*I could write something like this.*

But even as I thought it, something nagged at me.

*Where are the animals?*

I scrolled back through the book. I thought there'd been a mention of a dog, maybe. But nothing central to the story. I pressed my lips together.

If I was going to do this—if I was really going to pivot into romance—I couldn't leave animals behind. They were the whole reason I'd started writing. They were the thread that connected *Pawprints On Our Hearts* to Lexi's Legacy and to everything I cared about.

I typed a few notes into my laptop, keeping my movements small. Max was in my lap, his snout resting against my arm as he watched my fingers move across the keyboard.

I paused and looked down at him. "What do you think, boy? Think we can do this?"

He turned and studied my face for a moment, then stretched up and licked along my chin. It could've been because he smelled the pizza I'd had earlier.

Still, I smiled.

*"Look at my beautiful face. You're welcome for the inspiration."*

*"We're helping with research in our own way. Mind ya business."*

*Work + Book Research = This.*

*A new author friend at the conference.*

*"Scoot over. I got an idea ..."*

# 16

# Building the Plane

THE MONTHS THAT FOLLOWED blurred together. Days belonged to work. Nights belonged to the book.

I'd close my laptop around six, eat dinner with Crystal, and then reopen it around eight. The cursor would blink at me from a blank page, and I'd sit there until something came. Sometimes it took ten minutes. Sometimes it took two hours. But eventually, words came.

The story had already taken shape in my head: a small Southern town. A woman starting over. A rescue dog who needed her as much as she needed him. I could see the characters, hear their voices, and feel the world they lived in.

What I couldn't figure out was what to call it.

*Dog Days of Summer?*

*Too corny.*

*Second Chances?*

*Too vague.*

*Bark If You Love Me?*
*Horrible.*

I kept a running list in my notes app. Every few days, I'd add something new, stare at it, and hate it. The title would come eventually, I told myself. It had to. In the meantime, I wrote.

Some things felt familiar—the late nights, the doubt, and the way my back ached from sitting too long in the same position. I'd been here before with *Pawprints On Our Hearts*, and that muscle memory helped. I'd also known the ending because I'd lived it.

But fiction was different. With this novel, I was building the plane while flying it. Every scene led to another I hadn't written yet. Every choice my characters made opened up three more I hadn't considered.

*What would she say here?*
*Would he really do that?*

As I second-guessed everything, Max rotated between his bed and my lap. Spartacus mostly stayed in his own bed. After a while, I'd scoop up Spartacus and let him sit with me too; Max tolerated this arrangement with visible displeasure. Every hour or so, Crystal emerged.

"You need anything?"

"I'm good."

"Water?"

"I'm okay."

"Snack?"

"Maybe later."

She'd linger for a second, watching me type, then disappear again. Sometimes she'd come back with water anyway and set it on my desk without a word.

On a Sunday afternoon, I'd been staring at the same scene for an hour, with not much to show for it.

My main character was supposed to have a breakthrough moment that shifted her perspective and pushed her toward the love interest. I knew what needed to happen. I just couldn't piece it all together.

I typed a sentence. Deleted it. Typed another. Deleted that too.

*Come on.*

Behind me, Max and Spartacus had been wrestling for the past twenty minutes. They'd hauled both dog beds together, squaring off like rivals boarding each other's ships. They charged, retreated, then charged again in an endless back-and-forth, neither conceding an inch.

I watched, caught by it.

There was something almost enviable in the simplicity, and how the objective seemed so clear. The history nerd in me flashed to John Paul Jones aboard the *Bonhomme Richard*, refusing to surrender to the *Serapis*: *"I have not yet begun to fight."*

Part of me wanted to stay there a little longer, but this book wasn't going to write itself.

I cracked my knuckles and turned back to the screen. Instead of forcing the scene that wasn't coming, I skipped ahead to one I knew I'd need later. The words came easier than I expected. Lines began to stack and paragraphs formed.

Max darted past my feet, and Spartacus followed, nipping at his tail.

*Just one more paragraph.*

They collided with each other, tumbled, and ran every which way.

I'd typed half a sentence when I saw Max launch in my peripheral. He hit my lap and sprang onto the desk.

My water glass tipped, wobbled, and then—

*Splash!*

"Max!"

I yanked the laptop up, but it was too late. My jaw tightened as water dripped from the keys onto the desk, pooling around my notes.

Max leaped onto the floor and swished his tail as if this were some kind of game.

Spartacus meandered a few feet away.

I grabbed a shirt from the closet, wiped off the desk, and started dabbing at the keyboard.

*Of course.*

My gaze moved to the laptop, then to Max.

*Maybe it's a sign.*

Max's tail wagged harder.

I sighed and propped the laptop open in an upside-down triangle, hoping the water would drain. "Alright, boys. You win."

Crystal looked up from the couch when I came out of the office. Her eyebrows lifted. "He lives."

"Barely."

"What's wrong?"

"Max knocked water all over my keyboard."

She bit back a smile. "Is it okay?"

"Should be. Just letting it dry out."

"So you're done for the day?"

I glanced back at the office, then at the boys racing up and down the hall. "For a while."

Crystal's mouth curved. "They've been rowdy all weekend. Maybe we should try the new neighborhood dog park."

We stepped outside, and the late-spring air found me. I inhaled something sweet blooming nearby. The sun shone bright through the trees. A breeze moved through the branches, shaking loose a few stray petals that drifted down like confetti. A lawnmower hummed in the distance. A kid on a bike pedaled past, ringing a bell twice for no reason at all.

Max trotted ahead, convinced he was leading an expedition. Spartacus stayed close to Crystal, glancing up at her every few steps.

The park turned out to be farther than I'd expected. Far enough that the conversation thinned, then fell away altogether. Next time, we'd probably drive.

At one point, I looked over at Crystal as the light caught the freckles across her cheek and the bridge of her nose. A strand of hair fluttered in the wind, then settled again. She smiled, not at me exactly, just ... in my direction, without turning.

*This is good.*

I grabbed her hand, and the thought settled into me as we walked on.

Ahead of us, a small fenced-in area came into view, dotted with bright pops of color and a few benches. There were no other dogs or other people. Just us.

I pushed the gate open and ushered the boys through, then paused, giving the latch a tug. Then I double-checked, for good measure.

*Locked.*

"Feels great out here," Crystal said, unclipping Spartacus's harness.

"It does." I unclipped Max and stepped back, waiting for the explosion of energy.

Nothing happened.

They didn't run or sniff around. They stood there like a pair of stoic philosophers lost in apathy.

Crystal and I exchanged a look.

"Go on." I waved toward the open space. "Go play."

Max swept the park with his eyes—the fake red fire hydrant, the bright green agility tunnel near the back, and the water bowl clipped to a post. He flicked his gaze toward me and didn't move.

"Come on, boys." I reached into my pocket and pulled out the tennis ball we'd brought. I wound up and tossed it across the park. It bounced a few times and rolled to a stop by the back fence.

Both dogs watched it land. Neither chased it.

Spartacus sniffed the mulch near his feet, then walked to the gate and sat down.

Max followed. He lowered himself beside his brother, facing the exit, and looked up at me like, "Okay, so we're done here?"

Crystal pressed her lips together, but lasted maybe two seconds. "Look at them. We walked *all* the way over here."

I chuckled too. "They don't even care."

For a moment, I just stared at the two dogs sitting perfectly still at the gate of an empty park. Then, I walked over and grabbed the tennis ball. "Let's go."

The second we stepped through the front door, Max launched off the entryway tile, hit the living room rug at full speed, and tore a lap around the couch. Spartacus was right behind him.

They disappeared down the hallway toward my office.

I followed, still peeling off my shoes.

CRASH!

My stomach dropped.

I broke into a jog.

The laptop lay flat on the floor.

Max was on my desk, standing on a notebook.

"Maximus!"

He looked at me, then rolled over and began sniffing himself.

From his bed, Spartacus watched the scene unfold with detached interest.

I crossed the room in three steps, picked Max up off the desk, and set him on the floor. "That's a no-no."

He licked his nose and trotted away.

I turned back to the laptop and carefully lifted it upright. I checked the edges.

*No cracks.*

Tilted it toward the light.

*No scratches.*

I plugged it in, wiggled the cord, tapped the power button, and—

*Please still work.*

The screen flickered to life.

I exhaled.

Crystal appeared in the doorway and surveyed the scene, pursing her lips. "Yeah. So, I don't think they like the dog park."

*"We helped our daddy with a few chapters. Now it's nap time."*

*"Okay, so we're done here?"*

## 17

# Mr. Bestseller

**December**

*WOOF! WOOF!*

I blinked awake just as the bedroom door swung open and sunlight flooded the room.

"Hey, boys!" Crystal's voice carried from somewhere outside the room.

I squinted at the clock on the nightstand, but couldn't see it clearly.

The night before had gotten away from me. What had started as one quick game on the Switch turned into seven hours of Zelda, and a bowl of popcorn I definitely didn't share with Max or Spartacus. They had their own snacks.

Crystal leaned into the doorframe, still in her uniform from the medical office. She took one look at me, and the sheet twisted around my legs. "Came home early for lunch. Thought we could eat together."

I rubbed my eyes. "What time did you say it was?"

"I didn't." She laughed. "It's eleven though, Mr. Bestseller. Stayed up too late?"

I was yawning when my mind drifted back to the month before ...

The text had come through on a Wednesday.

I'd been watching a documentary about Roman aqueducts when my phone buzzed. I glanced down, expecting spam or maybe a shipping notification. Instead, I saw a picture from a friend.

My debut novel, *Since the Day We Danced*, featured in Times Square on a thirty-foot-tall digital billboard, glowing over the crowd. It read: *Instant #1 Bestseller*.

I sat up so fast Max tumbled off my lap.

*What?!*

I scrolled to the message above the image:

> Congrats! You hit #47 in the ENTIRE Amazon store. Not just #1 in your category. Out of millions of books, you're Top 50.

I read it again. Then again.

*Wild!*

I thought about the futon and the nights I'd wanted to quit and how I'd forced myself to keep going anyway. And now my book was in Times Square.

I immediately pulled up my royalty dashboard, expecting the usual trickle. What I saw made my breath catch.

*That can't be right.*

I refreshed the page.

Same number.

I did the math in my head: mortgage, bills, savings, and everything. Then I did it again, slower this time, making sure I wasn't missing something.

I wasn't.

*I could actually quit.*

On the rug, Max and Spartacus were rolling around, trading playful swats. My little co-authors were completely unaware that anything had changed, and something I couldn't quite describe began to move through me. Whatever it was, I let myself stay in it.

This was our moment.

That night, I told Crystal when we were in the kitchen. She was slicing vegetables for dinner.

I stood at the counter. "I think I'm quitting. Like, this week."

The knife stopped. She turned, and I saw her eyes already glistening before I'd even explained. "The book?"

I nodded. "It's enough. More than enough. I can write full time. Focus on Lexi's Legacy. Be here with the boys."

She set the knife down, crossed the space between us and wrapped her arms around me. "I'm so proud of you," she whispered.

At our feet, Max and Spartacus had gathered, tails wagging, like they knew something important was happening.

I looked down at our boys and smiled.

... "You getting up?"

The room came back to me.

"Just a minute."

I swung my legs over the side and sat there for a second, letting the grogginess fade. Then I shuffled to the bathroom and flipped on the light.

I leaned closer, examining my reflection. The grays had multiplied, and not just at my temples anymore, but through the top. I tilted my chin up. The skin beneath my jaw wasn't as tight as it used to be. Faint lines had settled around my eyes, deeper than I remembered.

*Thirty-six.*

I turned the faucet on and splashed water on my face.

*When did that happen?*

I straightened and looked again. The guy staring back at me looked tired.

I thought about the path that had led here and how I'd been responsible for teams of people since I was twenty-three.

*No wonder.*

I grabbed a towel and dried off.

For the first time in my adult life, no one needed me to show up anywhere. There were no shifts to cover or calls to join. No fires to put out.

I'd never felt lazier. And maybe that was okay.

I'd given so much for so long that the stress in my body had never fully left. Now, it finally had a place to go.

I needed these slow mornings and late nights playing video games with my dogs.

*January*, I told myself. After the holidays, I'll start writing the next book.

The fencing instructor raised her epee.

I adjusted my grip and bent my knees, feeling muscles I hadn't used in years.

Life had pushed hobbies like this aside, the way it tends to do. I'd fenced at the club level—nothing serious, but I'd loved it. It was like sword fighting without real risk. I'd considered getting back into MMA, but I wasn't twenty-two anymore. Fencing felt like the better choice.

The instructor lunged. I parried, and she pulled back with a small nod. "Not bad for your first day back."

I grinned beneath my mask.

"A little rusty," she said. "But we'll fix that."

By the end of the session, my legs burned, and sweat soaked through my jacket.

I hadn't felt this alive in months.

Christmas morning arrived, and by the time I stumbled into the living room, Max had already chewed through the paper and found what mattered.

Treats.

"Maximus Murray!" I kneeled beside him. "That's a no-no."

He looked up at me, a piece of tape stuck to his snout.

Spartacus sat nearby, watching his brother's mischief.

Crystal stepped in with two mugs of coffee and handed one to me. "Merry Christmas."

"Merry Christmas." I kissed her, took a sip, and watched the boys.

Max had abandoned the torn package and was now rounding the tree over and over, like a Roman chariot racer in the *Circus Maximus.*

Spartacus had finally moved closer, investigating a gift bag.

We spent the morning on the floor with them, opening presents and taking photos. Max got a new squeaky toy, and Spartacus got one too, though he didn't seem to care for it.

Later, after everything had been cleaned up, and the boys had worn themselves out, Crystal and I sank onto the couch. We turned on *It's a Wonderful Life,* and she leaned into me; I draped an arm around her.

On the rug, Max lay sprawled on his back, paws in the air, snoring. Spartacus was curled in his bed, eyes half-closed—except every few seconds, one would flutter open, then roll back again.

Crystal smirked. "Look at him. He looks possessed."

"Yeah. Kinda creepy. *Conjuring* vibes."

She stiffened, rolled her eyes back, and let her head tip to the side.

We both clamped our mouths shut, shoulders shaking.

"I've never seen you like this," Crystal whispered, still smiling.

I turned to face her. "Like what?"

"Happy. Actually happy."

*Forever grateful for my readers.*

*En garde!*

*"I love my giant carrot."*

*A Family Christmas.*

*"Oh, hi!"*

*"I've had better toys. Also worse ones."*

*"They got me the same toy as my brother, but I liked his better. He said I could have it."*

# 18

# Author Life

**Year Seven**

**2024**

IN THE KITCHEN, I started the coffeemaker and pulled out my notebook. While the machine gurgled, I jotted down the day's plan:

*8:30—CrossFit*
*10:00—Shower, breakfast*
*11:00—Write (2,000 words minimum)*
*1:00—Lunch and walk with the boys*
*2:00—Fan messages*
*3:00—Romance movie film study*
*5:00—Read*
*6:00—Family Dinner*

*8:00–Games*

*9:00—Bed*

The list wasn't a mandate. It was more like a suggestion I made to myself that kept me moving. I poured my coffee and took a sip.

*This is the life.*

The moment I grabbed my gym bag, Max's head shot up from the couch. Spartacus, who had been napping by the window, scrambled to his feet.

"I'll be back, boys."

Max launched off the cushion and sprinted, sliding the last few feet on the laminate. He planted himself directly in my path.

Spartacus took a different approach. He sat by the door and stared up at me with those big, pitiful eyes that said, "Didn't know you'd changed your name to Judas."

"Just an hour," I said, stepping over Max. "Maybe a little longer."

Sharp barks rang out.

I opened the door.

Both dogs shoved their noses into the gap, trying to squeeze through.

"Boys, stay."

I slipped out sideways, pulling the door shut behind me. *Click.*

From inside came the kind of screeching and squealing that would make a neighbor pause and reconsider what they'd just heard.

The CrossFit gym smelled like rubber and sweat. Large fans hummed overhead, and barbells clanked toward the back. I took in the room and realized most of the people there—many of them older than me—were fitter than I'd ever been. I made a mental note to ask about their routines.

I'd tried working out at home, but nobody told me home workouts weren't for dog dads. I'd bought dumbbells, resistance bands, and even one of those pull-up bars that hangs in a doorway.

It lasted three days.

During the first session, Max watched from his bed with mild curiosity. By the second, he'd decided my plank position was an invitation to play. My arms were already shaking and my core on fire when he jumped onto my back, knocked me flat, and started licking my face while I lay there.

In the third session, I attempted burpees. Max interpreted each jump as a game and started leaping alongside me. Spartacus tried to join in, launched himself once, landed, and immediately realized it wasn't for him. From there, he stationed himself beside the mat and began barking—encouragement, or maybe criticism. I'll never know. But by the end, I'd completed maybe twenty actual burpees and spent ten minutes wrestling two dogs off a yoga mat.

The memory faded, replaced by the instructor's booming voice. "Three ... two ... one ... go!"

The timer started, and I grabbed the barbell. Deadlifts. Then box jumps. Then rowing. The movements flowed together as my body worked and my mind wandered somewhere else entirely.

That was the thing about this new life. I could actually think now.

More book ideas floated up. Plot problems I'd been stuck on began to untangle themselves, and character motivations fell into place. By the time the timer buzzed, I'd mentally mapped out the next three scenes of my book.

I collapsed onto the mat, winded, staring at the ceiling. *Not bad for a Tuesday.*

I pulled into the driveway and cut the engine.

Through the front window, I saw two little faces pressed against the blinds. We'd given up on ever having nice ones. The moment my car door opened, I heard the rapid, percussive thud of a Yorkipoo-and-Morkie battering ram hitting the front door.

I walked up the path slowly, grinning.

When I stepped inside, Max hit my shins at full speed, bouncing off and circling back for another pass. Spartacus rose on his hind legs, pawing at my knees, tail whipping so fast I could barely track it. Both dogs made sounds that fell somewhere between barking and a squeaky grocery cart wheel.

I crouched. "I'm here, boys. I'm here."

Max licked my entire face in multiple swipes, while Spartacus nudged under my arm, demanding pets.

"Okay, okay." I stayed there, scratching behind both of their ears. "I missed you too."

When I finally stood and made my way to the kitchen, both dogs followed so close I nearly tripped twice. I grabbed a shaker bottle from the cabinet and mixed my peanut butter protein shake with almond milk.

As I took the first sip, a thought occurred to me.

*How long were they at that window?*

I pulled out my phone and opened our security app. We'd installed a few indoor cameras, not for safety reasons, but because watching the dogs while we were out had become a strange form of entertainment.

I scrolled back through the footage, scanning the time-stamps.

*8:15 a.m.* I leave.

On the screen, past-me walked out the door. Max and Spartacus stood still for approximately two seconds. Then they took off in frantic laps around the living room.

*9:04 a.m.*

They'd found the window. Max jumped onto the couch and pressed his face against the blinds. Spartacus joined him a moment later, squeezing into the narrow space between his brother and the armrest.

I fast-forwarded.

*9:15—Still there.*

*9:30—Still there.*

*9:45—Max shifted positions, but neither had moved more than a few inches.*

*10:00—Spartacus yawned.*

*10:15—Still there.*

*10:28—I pulled into the driveway. Both heads snapped to attention.*

I set my phone down, then squatted and rested a hand on each of them. "You didn't have to wait the whole time, boys."

I stood in front of the bathroom mirror, fixing my collar. I worked a small pinch of matte powder through my hair, coaxing it into something intentional, then leaned in closer to floss. I finished with a single spray of *Polo Red* cologne.

Behind me, Max and Spartacus watched from the bathmat.

I wasn't going anywhere. The farthest I'd travel today outside of our daily walk would be from the bedroom to my office; maybe twenty feet, if I took the long way through the kitchen.

Still, getting ready mattered.

*Look good, feel good, write good.* ("Write well" is the correct phrase here, but I think you know what I mean.)

The motto was a small thing, maybe even silly, but following it helped get my day going.

I smoothed down my shirt and nodded at my reflection one last time.

*I'm ready.*

Then—

A rustle next to me.

*Grocery bag.*

I turned just in time to see Max with his head buried in the bathroom trash.

"No-no, Maximus."

He froze, then slowly withdrew.

"Alright, boys." I clapped my hands twice. "Time to go."

In the office, I settled into my chair. Max and Spartacus followed me in and hopped onto their beds, which had drifted together beneath my desk.

*Pangea.*

Their little bodies were touching now. I smiled, then turned to the screen and clicked open my inbox. Fan messages had become one of my favorite and most surreal parts of the job.

*Dear Kerk, I just finished your book and I can't stop crying. My dog passed away last year, and your words helped me feel less alone.*

*Hi! I bought your book for my mom after she lost her golden retriever. She called me sobbing (in a good way) and said to thank you.*

*Your story inspired me to adopt a rescue. Meet Bruno!*

Attached was a photo of a terrier mix with one ear that stood up and one that flopped down.

After I responded to each one, I opened my manuscript and scrolled to where I'd left off yesterday.

*Chapter 14. The Beach.*

My fingers hovered over the keyboard.

*Okay. Let's do this.*

The words came slowly at first, then faster. I'd pause, read it back, fix what needed fixing, and keep going. By noon, I'd hit my goal: *2,147 words.*

I saved the document and pushed back from the desk. "Who wants to go on a walk?"

Every day, rain or shine, we took the same path. We passed the blue house with the yappy Chihuahua that exploded at the window and sent Spartacus into a fury. We rounded the corner where Max had once discovered a hamburger bun and scarfed it down before I could confiscate it. Then we crossed the cracked stretch of pavement and paused at the oak tree the boys insisted required a full cavity search every time.

I didn't listen to music or podcasts on these walks. I just watched the boys explore their world with a sense of wonder that never seemed to fade.

When we got home, playtime commenced. I'd drop to the carpet and roll back and forth like a steamroller, and they'd leap over me, toys clenched in their mouths. They brought me ropes, squeakers—anything they could find—urging me to grab on. We ended up in a pile on the toy-strewn floor, ready to eat.

Lunch came next. I'd make myself a sandwich and eat it on the couch, sometimes breaking off a small piece to share, though they knew better than to ask. They had their own routine: dog food left out in their bowls, a small carrot each, and a breath-freshening treat that bought me a few minutes of peace.

Then came the naps, all three of us sprawled across the living room in various states of unconsciousness. Max pressed against my side on the sectional. Spartacus had wedged himself along my legs. I lay back, with a book open on my stomach that I'd stopped reading thirty minutes earlier.

It wasn't a glamorous routine, and it wouldn't make for an exciting movie montage. But it was ours.

By the time fall arrived, we'd moved to Alabama—partly for adventure and partly because Savannah no longer felt as safe to live in as it once had. It was still a charming city, but living there revealed a different reality than passing through it.

We'd talked about it for months and weighed our options. Then one night, she looked at me and said, "What if we just left?"

Eight weeks later, we were unpacking boxes in Mountain Brook, a suburb just outside Birmingham.

The new home had more space, which the boys approved of. We needed it too. Back in the old house, boxes of paperbacks had taken over the office and then spilled into our bedroom. I'd started calling our bedroom "the warehouse," which Crystal did not find nearly as funny as I did.

Somewhere between writing full time and the move, I'd published two more books, *Since the Day We Fell* and *Since the Day We Kissed*. Each one hit a bestseller list and brought new readers, new messages, and new stories from people whose lives had intersected with mine through words on a page. And each one taught me something new about how much I still didn't know.

The more books I wrote, the more I saw what I could've done differently. Scenes I would've paced better. Dialogue I would've trimmed. Emotional beats I would've landed harder if I'd just trusted myself a little more.

It was maddening and exhilarating in equal measure.

I'd started reading four or five novels a month, mostly romances, but also memoirs and literary fiction and anything else that caught my attention. I studied them like game film, breaking down what worked and why.

Movies too. Ten romance films a month, minimum. I'd sit with a notebook and pause at key scenes, jotting down how they built tension or paid off a setup from act one.

Crystal had walked in on me once, rewinding the same thirty seconds of *Notting Hill* for the fifth time.

"Research," I'd said.

She'd just smiled and kept walking.

I took writing as seriously as Tom Brady took football. Maybe that sounds dramatic for a guy who writes love stories, but my readers deserved my best.

Growth was painful, and I made mistakes constantly. But I kept showing up, kept learning, and kept pushing.

I had the best job in the world.

The eight-foot table in my new office had disappeared beneath a mountain of books—hundreds of copies, fanned out in neat rows, waiting to be signed. Beside them were stacks of cardboard mailers, rolls of tape, and a pile of bookmarks.

Crystal sat next to me on our assembly line. We'd become a two-person fulfillment operation, spending entire evenings signing, wrapping, and packaging.

Below us, Spartacus watched from inside one of the canvas bags we used for post office runs. He'd climbed in twenty minutes ago and hadn't moved since.

"Only sixty-three left," she said, sealing another mailer.

"Only," I muttered, flexing my hand. My signature had devolved from *Kerk* to something closer to a heartbeat monitor reading.

I reached for the next book and stopped short.

Max was on the table, standing directly in the middle of the signing station.

"Maximus Murray." I set down my marker. "That's a no-no."

He ignored me and stepped across the surface, maneuvering between stacks. He paused at the pile of *Pawprints On Our Hearts* and lowered his head.

He sniffed the cover. Then he looked at the image of Spartacus's face printed across the front.

*Woof! Woof!*

I glanced at Crystal. She'd stopped wrapping, watching the scene unfold.

Max pawed gently at the stack, then looked up at me.

A whine this time.

I reached for him, and he let me scoop him up. I held him against my chest and looked into his eyes. "What's going on, boy?"

He licked my chin.

I grinned and glanced at the book cover. "You want to be on a cover too?"

He licked my face again.

I laughed and hugged him closer. "Okay, boy. I hear ya."

*"We're brothers obviously."*

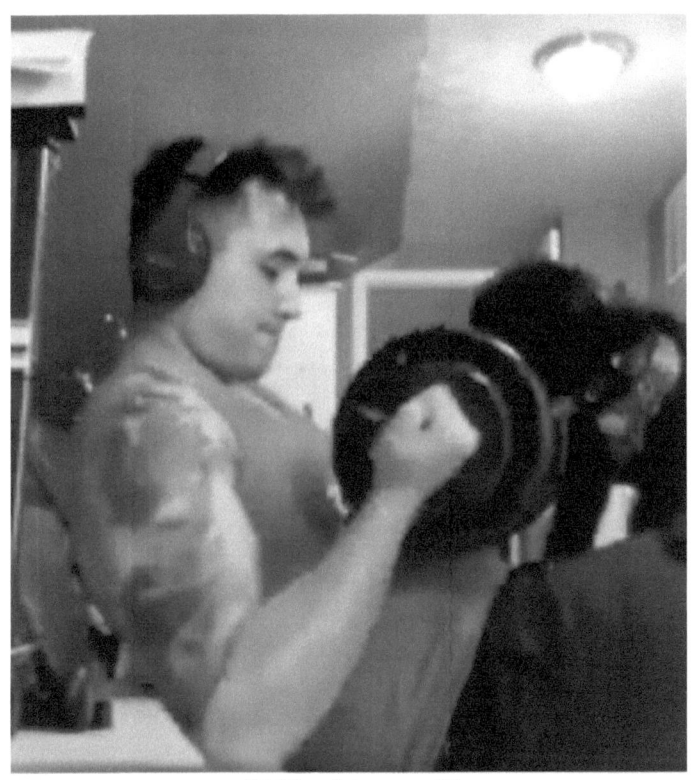

*"I like this game!"*

*"We weren't waiting the WHOLE time."*

*Finishing up the final draft of Since the Day We Kissed.*

*"So, when am I getting my own book?"*

*Since the Day We Kissed launch party!*

*"Why are you putting all this stuff in MY bag?"*

*"Dad's helping me write my book. How's Little Black Dog sound?"*

19

# Luckiest Man Alive

## August 2025

... "Earth to Kerk."

The words land in pieces.

I blink.

Cedar walls.

A mini-fridge buzzing.

The pan of banana muffins on the counter. Nearly empty.

I turn.

Crystal's standing by the window, arms crossed, smiling at me. "You okay?"

I look down at my hands, then back at her. "Yeah, just ... thinking."

"About?"

"Us. All of us."

She smiles.

At the door, scratching intensifies. High-pitched whines follow.

Crystal reaches for the leash bag. "Should we take them down to the water?"

I nod. "Let's do it."

For this trip, we'd brought the leashes that extend twenty feet or so, giving the boys room to run while still keeping them safe. In open spaces like this, it's the closest thing to freedom we can offer without risking Max bolting into the next county.

I clip Max's leash to his harness. He's already yanking me toward the door. "Hold on, boy."

Crystal secures Spartacus and gives me a look. "Ready?"

The air hits my face, cooler now than when we arrived. I can barely see the sun.

When we step off the deck, Max bursts onto the grass at full speed, leash unspooling behind him as he tears down the hill toward the water. I break into a jog to keep up. Then a run.

Max is a black blur ahead of me, legs churning, ears pinned back by the rush of air he's carving around him. The leash stretches to its limit, pulling at my hand. I pump my arms harder.

My legs aren't fast enough.

Behind me, I hear Crystal laughing—breathless, bliss-ful—and keeping pace with the lighter rhythm of Sparta-cus's paws against the ground.

Max glances back at me—only for a second—as if to say, "Faster, Daddy. Faster!"

I see it in the way he cuts back toward me, in the reckless joy radiating from every inch of his tiny body. He's not running away from me.

He's running *with* me. He's been doing it for seven years.

I push harder, lungs burning, legs screaming, and I feel something crack open inside me. Not pain. Something else.

*He's still fast. Still young enough to outrun me.*

The thought lands with a rush of fierce gratitude.

The grass gives way to the wooden slats of the dock, and I slow, legs wobbling, chest heaving. Max skids to a stop, tongue lolling, sides fluttering with happy breaths.

Crystal and Spartacus arrive moments later. She's dou-bled over, hands on her knees, laughing between gasps.

I'm bent over too, hands braced on my thighs, watching spots dancing at the edges of my vision.

Max sits at my feet, panting, looking up at me.

When my breathing finally steadies, I reach down and scoop Max into my arms. He settles against my chest, like he belongs there.

Crystal lifts Spartacus, and the four of us stand at the edge of the dock, facing the water.

The lake holds the lavender and gray of the sky. The sun is almost gone, and the faint outline of the moon is already there. A handful of stars has begun to show. Along the shoreline, frogs call to each other. Fireflies blink on in the tall grass, stitching small sparks of light into the dusk.

Across the way, I see the same group of people I'd noticed earlier. The kids are still splashing near the shore. The adults are gathered on a deck now. Someone laughs. The sound drifts toward us before dissolving into the evening air.

Neither of us speak.

I feel Crystal lean into me. Spartacus's head is drooping against her shoulder.

Max twists in my grip. He shifts his weight, turns his body, and suddenly we're face to face. Those dark eyes, the ones I've looked into a thousand times, find mine.

My throat tightens.

*Seven years.*

My mind slips somewhere I don't usually let it go:

A morning I haven't lived yet. The house without the jingle of tags. His bowl still in the corner, clean and dry. His red leash hanging by the door, untouched. The tiny indent in the couch cushion that used to hold his weight, barely there now.

I stop myself.

I know how this goes. But the thought doesn't scare me the way it once did. I don't push it away. I let it stay. Because loving him was never about how much time we'd ultimately get.

It's always been about showing up for *all* of it.

My eyes fill before I can stop them.

That little black dog doesn't know what he's done for me.

He just knows that I'm his. And he's mine.

The tears spill over. I don't wipe them away.

Max tilts his head, studying my face the way he always does when something's wrong.

But nothing's wrong.

I'm the luckiest man alive.

He leans forward and licks my cheek. Once. Twice. Then a third time, slower, like he's making sure he got it all.

A soft laugh slips out of me.

The fullness of something I can't quite name swells in my chest.

I pull him closer, pressing my forehead to his.

"I love you too, boy."

*"Faster, Daddy. Faster!"*

# Love this book? Don't forget to leave a review!

Help other readers discover *Little Black Dog*. Every review matters and it matters a lot. It can be as short as one phrase to a few sentences. Wherever you bought this book, you can use this link to leave an honest review on Amazon, Bookbub, Goodreads, or your favorite retailer:

**kerkmurray.com/products/reviewlittleblackdog**

# Get signed paperbacks up to 40% Off

**Bundle & Save at kerkmurray.com.**

*Apply this coupon at checkout
for an additional 10% off:* **MAX10**

The story of a boy whose life is saved by the love of dogs—and grows up to return the favor.

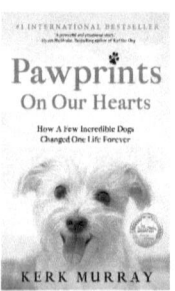

Escape to this small beach town, where heartfelt stories of love and redemption will make you laugh, cry, and believe in the magic of second chances.

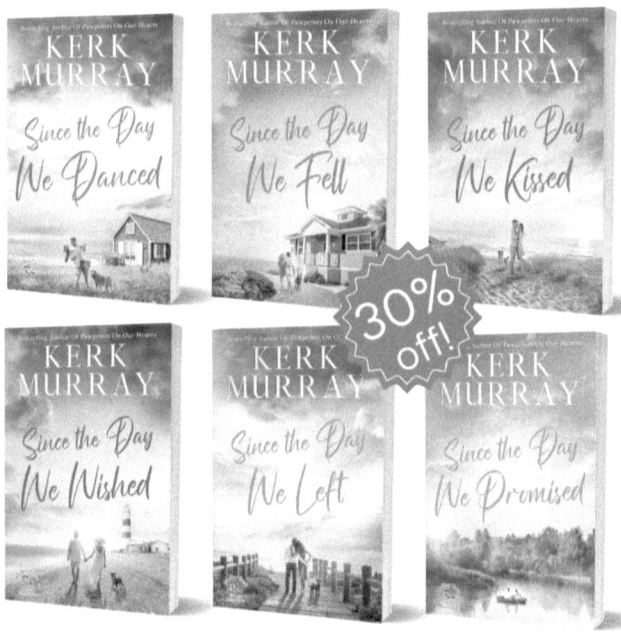

Welcome home to Sugarberry Ridge, where the greatest gifts aren't found under the tree—they're found in each other.

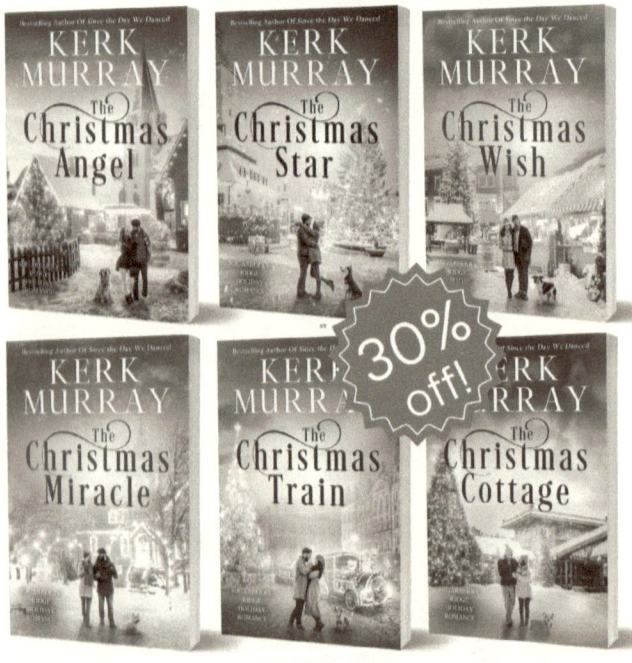

# Giving Back

"Never underestimate the power of a small group of committed people to change the world. In fact, it is the only thing that ever has."

—Margaret Mead

"Together redeeming the lives of animals and ending their suffering through our compassion."

THE LEXI'S LEGACY
FOUNDATION INC

Did you know a portion of my books' proceeds are donated to animal rescue organizations?

I'm so humbled that since 2020, my readers and donors and have helped raise nearly $300,000 in donations and services for animals in need.

If you feel compelled to donate, you can do so right here:

**donorbox.org/everydollarmatters**

Here's a list of the animal rescue organizations that readers are supporting monthly through each Kerk Murray book sale:

1. 2nd Street Hooligans Rescue – California

2. Cuddly – California

3. Little Hill Sanctuary – California

4. Love Always Sanctuary – California

5. Sale Ranch Animal Sanctuary – California

6. The Shore Sanctuary – California

7. Viva Global Rescue – California

8. Road To Refuge Animal Sanctuary – Connecticut

9. The Riley Farm Sanctuary – Connecticut

10. Love Life Animal Rescue & Sanctuary – Florida

11. Live Freely Sanctuary – Florida

12. Operation Liberation – Florida

13. SAGE Sanctuary and Gardens for Education – Florida

14. Farm of the Free – Georgia

15. Humane Society Greater Savannah – Georgia

16. Society of Humane Friends of Georgia – Georgia

17. Ruby Slipper Goat Rescue – Kansas

18. Shy 38 Inc. – Kansas

19. Sowa Goat Sanctuary – Massachusetts

20. Angela's Ark – North Carolina

21. Billie's Buddies Animal Rescue – North Carolina

22. Fairytale Farm Animal Sanctuary – North Carolina

23. Blackbird Animal Refuge – New Jersey

24. Broncs and Buns Rescue and Rehab – New Jersey

25. Fawn's Fortress – New Jersey

26. Happily Ever After Farm – New Jersey

27. Goats of Anarchy – New Jersey

28. Maddie & Sven's Rescue Sanctuary – New Jersey

29. Marley Meadows Animal Sanctuary – New Jersey

30. Old Fogey Farm – New Jersey

31. Rancho Relaxo – New Jersey

32. Runaway Farm – New Jersey

33. Troll House Animal Sanctuary – New Jersey

34. Wild Lands Wild Horse Fund – New Jersey

35. Happy Compromise Farm – New York

36. Sleepy Pig Farm Animal Sanctuary – New York

37. Woodstock Farm Sanctuary – New York

38. Enchanted Farm Sanctuary – Oregon

39. Harmony Farm Sanctuary – Oregon

40. Morningside Farm Sanctuary – Oregon

41. Charlie's Army Animal Rescue – Pennsylvania

42. Happy Heart Happy Home Farm & Rescue – Pennsylvania

43. The Philly Kitty Club – Pennsylvania

44. The Misfit Farm – Texas

45. Best Friends Animal Society – Utah

46. Harmony Farm Sanctuary and Wellness Center – Vermont

47. Off The Plate Farm Animal Sanctuary – Vermont

48. Gentle Acres Animal Haven – Virginia

49. Little Buckets Farm Sanctuary – Virginia

# Visit Lexi on
# the Rainbow Bridge

Lexi always loved to make new friends! Be sure to sign her guestbook! You can visit her virtual memorial at

**rainbowsbridge.com/residents/LEXI032/Residen t.htm**

# About the Author

Kerk Murray is an Amazon Top 50 and Barnes & Noble bestselling author of clean contemporary romance. His series include *Dog Lovers*, *Hadley Cove Sweet Romance*, and *Sugarberry Ridge Holiday Romance*.

Fans of Rachel Hanna and Debbie Macomber will love his Southern small-town stories about second chances—featuring swoony heroes, strong heroines, and rescue animals that you'll fall in love with too.

Beyond writing, Kerk is the founder of *The Lexi's Legacy Foundation*, a 501(c)(3) nonprofit that helps animal rescues save more lives. A portion of his book proceeds supports this mission because every animal deserves a forever home.

Connect with Kerk and sign up for his newsletter at **kerkmurray.com** for new releases and exclusive sneak peeks of upcoming books.

For film and subsidiary rights inquiries: **info@kerkmurray.com**

**a** Kerk Murray

**g** Kerk Murray

**BB** @kerkmurray

**f** @kerkmurrayauthor

**O** @kerkmurray